BLACKBALLED TWICE

By Mike Norris

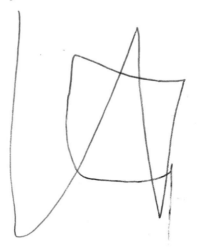

Photo Credits:

Muhammad Ali – Photographer Gordon Parks 1970
Mike Norris – page 11, The Trading Card Database
Mike Norris – page 17, Cliff Welch / Icon Sportswire
Curt Flood – Public Domain
Rickey Henderson – en.wikipedia.org
Dave Winfield – AP Photo
Tony Gwynn – Baseball Hall of Fame
Mo'ne Davis – Charles Krupa / Associated Press
Mike Norris – page 65, Topps
Mike Norris – page 74, Mother's Cookies
Mike Norris – page 142, Mother's Cookies
Jackie Robinson – US Information Agency 1950
Mike Norris – page 149, Fleer
Mike Norris – page 177, Topps
Barack Obama – Photo by Pete Souza 2012 P120612PS-0463
Mike Norris – page 182, Topps
Back Cover – Andy Hayt / Getty Images

Edited by: Shari Bruce
Book layout by: Shari Bruce
Cover design by: Shari Bruce
Published by: Sistahs With Ink Foundation

Printed in the United States of America

ISBN-13:978-1546518204

ISBN-10:1546518207

DEDICATION: MUHAMMAD ALI's VICTORY AND DEMOCRACY

This man was intrinsically associated with boxing universally. He, as well as we, referred to him as the greatest of all times. Against the U.S. Army, he was a fighter outside the ring and a boxer inside the ring, when the bell rang—ding! He made you anticipate and wait to hear him guesstimate through a rhyme on how he was going to "whip his opponent this time."

His integrity was second to none, that's why he didn't enlist to go to Vietnam to use a gun. In one of his many infamous and profound quotes, he stated, "Them Vietnamese ain't never called me Nigger." That's why he didn't enlist in the Army, so he wouldn't have to pull that murderous trigger. Was it his faith or was it his belief keeping him strong up underneath? As he became a conscientious objector, the Nation of Islam became his protector, and the great Malcolm X became his preceptor.

On February 25, 1964 22 years after his birth in Louisville, Kentucky and a year before his rebirth as Muhammad Ali, Cassius Clay beat Sonny Liston to become the Heavyweight Champion of the World. After the refusal of being drafted into the Army, the next three and a half years of his life would be imperiled. He was stripped of his title, with no sense of immediate income, and that became extremely vital. His fight was not only for the government, but it was with the boxing commissioners and politicians. Sometimes on their own, sometimes under the pressure of veteran's groups, the press and various self-appointed protectors of our "national honor."

The Ali ban was originated by Edwin Dooley, who was the president of the New York State Athletic Commission. During the afternoon of April 28, 1967 a few hours after Ali had formally refused induction but before he had been charged with a crime, Dooley announced that Ali's license to box in New York had been "indefinitely suspended" because of "his refusal to enter the service was regarded by the commission to be not in the best interests of boxing." Boxing commissioners around the country quickly copied New York.

It was in exile that Ali grew into a powerful symbol of Black struggle. By late 1967, *Ebony* magazine noted that Ali's "popularity seemed to have increased."

Then in 1967 came the dissent from Martin Luther King Jr. who decided that peace in Vietnam and progress in Civil Rights were causes inextricably intervened. King had died before the killing stopped in Vietnam, but his year of opposition reached deep into the Black community. He put a new perspective on the war, which probably led many to view Ali's opposition in a new light. King repeatedly endorsed Ali's refusal to fight. In speeches encouraging conscientious objectors, King told his audiences to admire (Ali's) courage. He is giving up fame. He is giving up millions of dollars to do what his conscience tells him is right.

As an increasing number of Blacks developed an aversion to the Vietnam War, Ali began expressing his anti-war stance in a secular vocabulary that resonated with Black Americans beyond the Nation of Islam. In court, he depended solely on his religious beliefs to justify his draft resistance. But in speeches and interviews during his exile, a dichotomy emerged in his reasons for opposing the war.

"If I thought going to war would bring freedom, justice, and equality to 22 million American Negroes in America, they wouldn't have had to draft me; I'd join tomorrow."

In November 1969, Ali's lawyers finally brought the question of his right to box into the judicial arena by filing a lawsuit against Edwin Dooley and the NYSAC for revoking Ali's license. His lawyers claimed that the commission arbitrarily punished the client while on several occasions licensing [other] professional boxers, notwithstanding evidence of such individuals would be far more likely to be detrimental to the interest of boxing than the plaintiff. His claim was initially rejected by the federal district judge for lack of evidence.

After the dismissal, Ali's lawyers laboriously searched through New York States' criminal records and found more than 200 instances of convicted felons, being licensed by the NYSAC; men convicted of robbery, arson, rape, second-degree murder, and desertion of the armed forces had been allowed to box by the NYSAC. Considering the new evidence, Ali was granted a new hearing. This time they ruled in his favor; Ali had regained the right to fight.

Simultaneously, with the lawsuit against the NYSAC, supporters and promoters continued searching the country, supplicating cities and their officials to allow Ali to fight. Finally, in the least likely of places, a city was found willing to submit itself to media condemnations and politician's recriminations. Atlanta, in the middle of the South, the domain of segregationist Governor Lester Maddox, agreed to an ostracized Black boxer the opportunity to fight. The city's liberal Jewish mayor withstood pressure from several sides and honored an agreement to let Ali fight Jerry Quarry in October 1970. At the time, the deal was made between Ali and Atlanta, the outcome of his case against the NYSAC was still much in doubt. As it turned out, he won his case September 1970. After a 42-month layoff, he won the fight in October.

On April 19th, 1971, Chauncey Eskridge argued before the Supreme Court that Muhammad Ali was a legitimate conscientious objector, forbidden to fight by a religion in which he fervently believed. Two months later, the court declared a winner in Clay vs. the United States, a unanimous decision for Muhammad Ali.

Muhammad Ali, you were my idol although the Bible says, "Thy shall not have no other God before me." I wanted to grow up and be like you and be the greatest of all times too! You were bigger than life, a Black prodigy and that's no hyperbole. To my knowledge, you were the first Black man to publicly brag and have super swag. You were highly impressive and had an attention-attracting style. You spoke in a shower of lyrical self-praise and rhyming bravado with guts and guile. You told anyone who would listen that you were the prettiest, the wittiest, and the greatest. To me, the greatest consisted of the biggest, brightest, smartest, coolest, realest, surest, toughest, bluntest, and probably most importantly, the nicest. When I heard you say after defeating Sonny Liston for the Heavyweight Championship of the World, "I am the greatest, I'm the Heavyweight Champion of the World. I'm just 22 years old, I must be great. *I talk to God every day and if He's for you, who can be against you?" Romans 8:31* As a 9-year-old boy, what he said I believed to be true. What I got the most out of that was that my faith in God exponentially grew. From there I took those ten adjectives and applied them to my life. Then later as an adult, I found that without them it brought about some severe strife.

I've just turned 20 years old and became the 35th pitcher in Major League Baseball to throw a shutout in their debut. Muhammad, before every game I pitched, I mentally and physically brought you from within me. My approach was that the opposing team was my enemy; that sounds more like a boxer's mentality. After the game, I was being interviewed, and it took every bit of my power not to say I shook up the world, I'm just 20 years old, I must be great! If God is for me who can be against me?

Before the game, I spar and shadow box for close to an hour, while hollering, "Rumble young man, rumble," even after the game, and if I won, even in the shower! When I'm all alone in the clubhouse, I'm shouting, "I'm the greatest of all times, there will never be a pitcher that can do what I do, of all times."

I find myself surrounded by stars and even superstars such as Reggie Jackson, Vida Blue, Campy Campaneris, Sal Bando, Gene Tenace, Rollie Fingers and a young rising star who in the minors was my close friend and roomie, Claudell Washington, in AA. Upon leaving, he was only supposed to go up for 15 days, but before walking out that door, he said, "Norris, I'm not coming back!" After Claudell played good enough to stay, for me, he just paved the way. The very next spring training I made the team by bypassing AAA. This is a team that just finished winning their 3rd World Series in succession. Vida Blue, who is a close friend, has left a life-long impression. When one of the local media asked was I intimidated by all the stars? With no filter or discretion, I replied, "The only stars are in the sky." Some of the veterans felt I was too cocky and was headed in the wrong direction. But clearly it was I, doing my version of Muhammad Ali and they soon found out that they had the wrong perception. Muhammad, like you, I was second to none when it came to athletic prowess, as we were supremely blessed with both power and finesse.

Then there was that period in my life, that drugs and alcohol became my strife! I took a page out of your book to show my courage, to become encouraged and not get overwhelmed and become discouraged. Coincidently, we spent 3-4 years in exile losing millions of dollars in the prime of our lives; witnessing our careers taking a dive (no pun intended). The duplicitous actions of politicians, commissions, and commissioners was motivated and based on race and religion. Was the U.S. government afraid and intimidated by Ali's Islamic conversion? This led to bias conversations, accusations, derisions, fatal rescissions, and unfair decisions.

Through the grace of God, we survived and thrived. Of course, Muhammad regained his greatness and became a 3-time heavyweight champion of the world. His career ended at 39 years old to a defeat by Trevor Berbick, as that was one of the five total losses against fifty-six wins out of sixty-one fights, thirty-seven, by way of knockout. Perhaps the most famous of all his fights as that proved to be the rebirth of his legacy, the three fights with "Smokin' Joe" Frazier, who held the heavyweight championship belt during Ali's vacancy. With Ali losing the first fight, winning the second, and the last fight billed as the "Thriller in Manila" to gain back his championship belt. Oh, how awesome that must have felt! But as he got older, the fast hands and the quick feet, he was no longer the beholder. His next opponent was "Big George" Foreman who appeared to be even bolder as if he could knock your head off your shoulders. He defeated the relentless Joe Frazier by knocking him literally up and down in the ring until the bell rang ding.

The fight between Ali and Foreman took place in Zaire, Africa. The only way I could see him beating Big George would have to be a heavy accumulation of bee stings. Many Ali fans didn't have much faith or hope, but Ali's brilliant gamesmanship came up with the "rope-a-dope." He went from his opponent missing while swinging at the air, to a wiser and older boxer lying on the ropes and absorbing Big George's brutality—it was as if it didn't hurt or care. It was like an out-of-body experience as if he wasn't there. Round after round he punched Ali so much and so hard, he experienced total fatigue. Next came round eight and Ali came off the ropes with a five-punch combination that sent Big George reeling. That would be the last that he would see of the rope-a-dope, as he lost his balance, staggered, and lurched forward. It was as if he fell on a bar of soap. In my point of view, this fight embodied and solidified his greatness through mind over matter, as he slew and cut off Big George's head and put it on a platter (a figure of speech). This fight was appropriately named the "Rumble in the Jungle." By 1981, Big George and Muhammad became the best of friends. Foreman eventually concluded, "Ali is the greatest man I ever known, not the greatest boxer, that's too small for him. He had a gift. He's not pretty, he's beautiful! Everything America should be, Muhammad Ali is."

Muhammad, I'm counting all the incredulous characteristics that I took from you, and then I applied them in resourceful ways, which assisted in me having very productive days. You gave me the drive and ability to ameliorate egregious situations. While learning, a man has got to know his limitations.

The greatest man that walked this earth was wrongly crucified and died. Muhammad Ali, you were the next greatest to walk this earth and you were revered and idolized, and like Jesus, you totally optimized. But I have no sorrow, only hope for tomorrow, because they both embodied love beyond reasons and throughout all seasons

RIP MUHAMMAD ALI

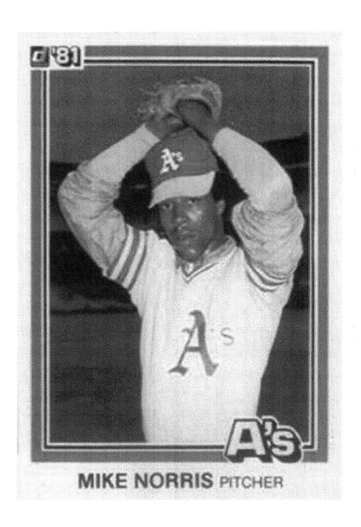

SARCOIDOSIS, THE MYSTERIOUS HEALTH THREAT

The disease of Sarcoidosis is the growth of tiny collections of inflammatory cells in different parts of your body. Most commonly the lungs, lymph nodes, eyes, and skin. Join me and many others to fight this mysterious health threat and eventually win. Sarcoidosis sometimes develops gradually and produces symptoms that last for years. Other times symptoms appear suddenly and then just disappear. There's no cure for Sarcoidosis. But most people do well with modest treatment. Alternatively, signs and symptoms of Sarcoidosis lead to organ damage, which can result in death and bereavement. Doctors believe Sarcoidosis results from the body's immune system, responding to an unknown substance, most likely something inhaled in the air. With all the pollutants, viruses, dust, chemicals, and specific bacteria, gaining this knowledge will make you much more aware.

I learned about Sarcoidosis with much intrigue; weight loss, fever, swollen lymph nodes, resulting in exhausting fatigue. Almost everyone who has Sarcoidosis eventually experiences lung problems, a persistent cough, shortness of breath and wheezing. To say the least, this doesn't sound too pleasing.

As many as 25% of the people who have Sarcoidosis develop skin problems, which may include rash, lesions, color change, and nodules, which are growths just under the skin, that may develop particularly around scars and tattoos. To go through all of this, one must be brave and exhibit a super-positive attitude.

Then there are the eye symptoms. Sarcoidosis can affect eyes without causing any symptoms. So, my suggestion to you is to have your eyes checked. Find out through an eye test what your doctor can detect. When eye symptoms do occur, you could become sensitive to light, have severe redness, eye pain and blurred vision. After learning of the effects, getting your eyes checked shouldn't be such a difficult decision!

In Sarcoidosis, some immune cells collect in a pattern of inflammation called granulomas. As granulomas build up in an organ, the function of that organ can be affected. Normally your immune system helps protect your body from foreign substances and invading organisms such as, bacteria and viruses that get rejected. While anyone can develop Sarcoidosis, factors that may increase your risk include age and sex.

Sarcoidosis often occurs between the ages of twenty to forty. Women are more likely to develop the disease. Race—personally, this is what reached out and slapped my face! African-Americans have a higher incidence of Sarcoidosis than do White Americans. Also, Sarcoidosis may be severe and may be more likely to recur and cause lung problems in African-Americans. Family history—if someone in your family has had Sarcoidosis, you are more likely to develop the disease yourself.

For the most part, Sarcoidosis can be long lasting (chronic) in some people and lead to complications that may affect different parts of the body. African-Americans must deal with this disease to appease. We must approach this with vigorous and rigorous research and then committing to siege. This is serious if it gets in your lungs. Untreated, pulmonary Sarcoidosis can lead to the tissue between the air sacs in your lungs, making it extremely difficult to breathe. Eye inflammation can affect almost any part of your eyes and eventually can cause blindness. Rarely, Sarcoidosis can cause cataracts and glaucoma. Kidney Sarcoidosis can affect how your body handles calcium, which could lead to kidney failure. Heart granulomas within your heart can interfere with the electrical signals that drive your heartbeat causing abnormal heart rhythms, and in rare instances death!

Nervous system, a small number of people with Sarcoidosis develop problems related to the central nervous system. When granulomas form in the brain and spinal cord, inflammation in the facial nerves could cause facial paralysis. This disease has taken lives and afflicted some very infamous celebrities. These celebrities include: Bernie Mac, Reggie White, and Mahalia Jackson. The knowledge of them passing left me in shock and confusion. Tisha Campbell-Martin has also been afflicted and is in remission. That's the latest I have on her condition.

Below are two lists of celebrities that are currently afflicted or have passed from this mysterious disease:

Afflicted:

Bill Russell	Professional Basketball Player
Floyd Mayweather Sr.	Professional Boxer and Trainer
James A. Ray	Professional Basketball Player
Angie Stone	Recording Artist, Producer, and Actress
Karen Duffy	Model, Television Personality, and Actress
Daisey Fuentes	Television Host, Comedian and Model
Tisha Campbell-Martin	Actress and Singer
Travis Michael Holder	Actor and Playwright

Deceased:

Mahalia Jackson	Gospel Singer
Manning Marable	Professor and Author
Bernie Mac	Comedian
Drew Stein	Stop Sarcoidosis Member
Reggie White	Professional Football Player
Darrian Chapman	NBC5 Sportscaster
Sean Lavert	R&B Singer
Daniel W. Stoddard	Found Sarcoidosis Life
Daryl Hawks	NBC5 Sportscaster
Michael Clark Duncan	Actor and Voice Actor

It doesn't matter about your race, creed, sex, or your denomination, this disease doesn't practice discrimination. Eventually it can contribute to your elimination. So, don't be guilty for exercising procrastination, just go and see your doctor for your own clarification! We're up against a tough fight, so we must walk by faith and not by sight. A cure is in the near future and it looks extremely bright.

When you do see your doctor he or she will likely start you off with a physical exam, including a close examination of any skin legions you may have. Your doctor will also listen carefully to your heart and lungs and check your lymph nodes for swelling. Your doctor may also be interested in seeing previous chest X-rays to see if early signs of Sarcoidosis were overlooked. Again, make an appointment today, you want to get in as soon as you can with very little or no delay. Diagnostic tests can help exclude other disorders and determine what body systems may be affected by Sarcoidosis. Your doctor may recommend X-rays, CT scan, PET or an MRI, blood test, lung function test and an eye exam. So, join me as we talk that talk and confidently walk that walk.

Let's be motivated by these very significant quotes:

"You don't have to be great to start but you have to start to be great." *Zig Ziglar*

"The wise does at once, what the fool does last." *Baltasar Graciàn*

"We're hitting the ground running." *President Obama*

"Walk by faith and not by sight." *Hebrews 11:1*

This poem is dedicated to a very special woman, Ann Weaver for her thoughtful and charitable giving. Daughter Dr. Angela Wheeler has enhanced the Ann Weaver Foundation through her very own creation.

Growing up, she experienced her mother going through immense pain and misery.
That was the daily existence of her plight.
Eventually she succumbed with incredible bravery, dignity and class.
All the way to the final bell, she put up a good fight.
She didn't need an invitation to heaven
She already earned her pass
As she was the Heavenly Father's sacrifice
So let me share some good advice
With all the help from your heartfelt prayers, through being informed, educated and much needed donations
We can become the West Coast hub
And continue to grow and prosper across the nation
Through the Heavenly Father the entire world can be our final destination.

Since this information was so extensive, I put it in the form of a poem to make it a little more enjoyable and comprehensive.

Join the fight!

https://www.t25cl.com/pages/ann-weaver-foundation

INTRODUCTION - CLARITY ABOUT ME

In 1973, Mike Norris was a first-round draft choice, 24th pick in the nation by the Oakland A's. He became the 35th pitcher in major league history to throw a complete game shutout in his major league debut.

In 1980, he won 22 games and lost 9. Completed 25 games out of 33 starts. Also, was the Cy Young Award Runner-Up. Mr. Norris became 1 of 15 African-American pitchers in the history of Major League Baseball to win 20 games or more in one season – earning him entrance into an elite group called "The Black Aces."

In 1981, Mike Norris made the American League All-Star Team. He is one of 127 players to play for one team for ten years or more. He also made a historic comeback in 1990. No one has been out of the major leagues over four years and made a comeback since WWII. Mike Norris' career-win record was 60 wins and 60 losses.

1. WHO IS GOD?

Due to the repetitive use of the word or name "God" I would to like to take the time to address those who may not share in the belief of God. Or that their respected religion has another name for the Supreme Being. I'm merely compromising when I choose to use the name Heavenly Father, because in no way shape, fashion, or form are my intentions to neither insult nor offend my most appreciated readers.

The dictionary's definition of God is a supreme being, an almighty being, and the principal object of faith. He's the creator and the ruler of the universe. Faith is trust and confidence in complete acceptance of a truth that cannot be demonstrated or proven by the process of logical thought.

When you are talking about God, some people ask, if they are not a believer, how do you know there is a God. You can't prove it. That's where faith comes in. You tell them your experience with repenting, getting baptized in Jesus' name, and receiving the gift of the Holy Spirit, and that's your proof. This is just another way of God bringing you the gospel truth.

Here are some wonderful quotes and biblical scriptures about the significance of faith:

1. Beginnings are usually scary and endings are usually sad, but it's the middle that counts. You must remember this when you find yourself at the beginning.
Sandra Bullock

2. God didn't promise days without pain, laughter, or sorrow, sun without rain, but he did promise strength for the

day, comfort for the tears, and light for the way. If God brings you to it he will bring you through it. *Unknown*

3. Faith is believing in something when your common sense tells you not to. From the movie, *"Miracle On 34th Street"*

4. Faith is taking the first step, even when you don't see the whole staircase. *Martin Luther King Jr.*

5. Just because you can't see it doesn't mean it isn't there. You can't see the future, yet you know it will come; you can't see the air, yet you continue to breathe. *Claire London*

6. Faith is the substance of things hoped for and the evidence of things not seen. *Hebrews 11:1*

7. For we walk by faith and not by sight. *2 Corinthians 5:7*

8. And Jesus said unto them, because of your unbelief: for verily I say unto you, if ye have faith as a grain of mustard seed, ye shall say unto this mountain, remove hence to yonder place; and it shall remove; and nothing shall be impossible unto you. *King James Bible*

———————————————————————————

So, this is what we need to do with our faith. We don't need to just believe in God, we need to belong to everything about God. Believe that He will forgive all your sins. Believe He will give you the Holy Spirit. Believe that His only begotten son died on the cross for your sins. Believe that He rose from the dead and ascended back into Heaven. Believe that we will praise Him forever and if you don't believe what's been said, your hell will be a lake of burning fire. So, your best choice is to serve God, that should be your heartfelt desire! Love Him with all your heart and soul and put Him first in your life. That means before your job, children and even your wife.

To start your day, I suggest you set some time aside, so you can pray! When you do pray, believe it and claim it, things most likely will turn out into a positive way. God made ten commandments on how you should live every day. When you do come up short and sin, that evil entity called Satan, counts that as a win. As humans, this may seem and feel odd, but as much as he is almighty, he's a forgiving God. Reading the Bible is for knowledge, nourishment and time well spent. As you will learn, when you sin, all you must do is repent. God promises that your sin is totally forgotten, because after you sin, you usually feel rotten. Without God in your life, you're destined for trouble and lots of strife. God doesn't want you to be broke and spiritually deceased. He wants you to have life in abundance with total increase. He doesn't want you to live in hopeless addiction. Just pray to him and he can remove that affliction. Don't be depressed, God has joy that can turn sad to glad. He can remove and heal any problem, while enjoying it, I might add. Some may call his blessings a miracle or impossible, but it's something you can't deny nor suppress. You don't have to look for an answer, just realize that you've been blessed.

So, in conclusion, this is the most significant information you must possess.

"For God so loved the world that he gave his only begotten Son, that whoever believes in Him would not perish, but have everlasting life." *John 3:16*

Now this is some powerful advice,
this was meant to make you think twice.
Please don't go to church Sunday
and sin all week starting Monday,
that's being a hypocrite.
So if that's what you're doing—you need to quit.
The book of Genesis starts in the beginning and the back
is Revelation in the end, and in that time there will be the
battle of Armageddon and God wins.
God gives you what you need in order to succeed.
Thank Him for your health and monetary proceeds.
You must have faith which means to believe
blessed to achieve and receive.
As you'll be blessed to achieve that diploma, job, wife, and
all the healthy children she can conceive,
you deserve to receive.

2. BLACKBALLED AND LABELED

The act of being blackballed and labeled is equivalent to being mentally and physically disabled, some reference this to paralysis or incapacitated as a vegetable. This punitive action is designed for permanent closure of your career. Now blemished and tainted from the recreational and illegal usage of cocaine and my alcoholism producing of a couple of DUI's, but still attempting to continue on a course of action even in the face of difficulty in my sobriety. With no prospects of success, one must persevere!

"I can do all this through Him who gives me strength."
Philippians 4:13

"Let us throw off everything that hinders and the sin that so easily entangles. And let us run with perseverance the race marked out for us." *Hebrews 12:1*

Blackballing can't be detected, and there's no one to be held accountable. Many have sued Major League Baseball over such things in the past; over minimum wage violations and collusion. The antitrust exemption has been filed and ultimately lost. Barry Bonds is the latest to sue Major League Baseball for collusion instead of filing a grievance.

Collusion results when companies (in this case teams) get together to make secret agreements that are possibly unethical or illegal. So how can this be detectable or debatable when to most, unless it happens to you, isn't comprehensible? That's the only thing that's understandable. Is it plausible or could it be possible? One thing is for sure it will never be chronicled, or will it just be another story told? Well, believe me, because this is believable. What is this all about, there's no doubt on who has the clout, when they can literally but illegally put you out? If they wouldn't let the home run king play, shouldn't we be in the least dismay?

What comes next wasn't even conceivable but applicable. This was definitely something outside the box and very unconventional. Once a player is blackballed, his chances of returning to baseball are none and void, which is quite predictable. Will the organization be held accountable for their actions that are highly questionable? The action they took was over an insurance policy with a very reputable company for millions of dollars. All they had to prove was that my career ended because of arm troubles and the insurance company's defense was that my career ended because of a cocaine addiction! As I'm quite sure, the team took out as much, if not considerably more, than I had on my right arm for five million dollars. To the organization that was obviously a major temptation and most desirable.

After being out of baseball for roughly four years, I had plenty of time to reflect on my career and many a day I shed a few tears. Looking back, it wasn't very clear and looking ahead there was plenty of fear.

After playing summer baseball in Mexico, according to competition and status, I hit bottom, and that was low. After about two weeks of eating at the same place I decided to eat elsewhere, I believe I chose chicken on the menu. There is a stomach virus that you can get from eating spoiled meat; therefore, you must watch where you eat. The name of this gastrointestinal upset is called *Montezuma's revenge* which is a food poisoning that lasts three days. By day two, you're just asking God to take you, as you experience extreme diarrhea and vomiting. You become very weak and dehydrated as you just lay on the bathroom floor. You are unable to make it back to your bed as your body just can't take it anymore. Finally, day three arrived, after recovering; I gave into my flesh as I had enough and explained to the team the reason for my departure.

I returned home, a week passed, and I felt as if I had been put out to pasture. This felt too much like failure. I couldn't picture living my life out as the victim and not the victor. Now I had to adhere to my advice, which is winners never quit and quitters never win! I've always persevered when it came to saving my career. I had to decide was I going to hide or make a phone call and swallow my pride? Will I again be denied or extremely satisfied?

After a heartfelt conversation that consisted of me being humble, appreciative, and accountable, the GM agreed that I had paid enough dues; in hindsight, I didn't detect deception or any other similar clues. Wow, unreal, I was getting another chance; I was so excited I thought I was going to need an ambulance. Although through my acquisition, I wasn't aware that I would need to take a deposition. Well, the organization apparently won the deposition, and I signed an AAA contract and went to spring training starting the season in AA. In only one start I illustrated that I certainly didn't belong there as I tossed a two-hit shutout over six innings. The manager was Jeff Newman who was my catcher during the best years of my career.

The following day, he called me into his office with a look of disgust and disappointment as if I had flunked a random drug test that was required. I asked, "What's wrong?" and without changing his facial expression, he said, "You're going to AAA." In a matter of moments my emotions went from fear to joy, and now I'm just one step away. On a parting note, he told me that was the same stuff I had in the big leagues. That sent me on my way with more confidence and intrigue.

I was extremely pumped up for my first start in AAA as I proceeded to go out and throw a masterful and typically complete game shutout. But this style of pitching complete games led to my almost career ending surgery; I'm only concerned about getting back to the big leagues with urgency. In retrospect, that wasn't very good strategy, as in my next start I had arm fatigue. This is when your arm doesn't hurt, but your fastball has no velocity. Now after 5 losses, I was demoted to the bullpen, so I could throw more frequently to build arm strength. That proved to be a good move, and eventually, I moved back into the starting rotation as I went five and one the rest of the way, winding up 6-6 with a 354 ERA. To my disappointment, I wasn't even called up to the show, not even after the expansion of the 40-man roster. I had endured and accomplished a lot, so there was no reason to hang my head. All that will do is create bad posture.

Around Christmas, they send out contracts, and through the grace of the Heavenly Father, I received a big league contract. Spring training comes, and I have a brilliant spring, I make the team but I come to learn not quite everyone is pulling for me. The organization had changed as far as I could see, there wasn't even a hint of the Billyball regime. There was no doubt this was Tony La Russa's team. I found this out the hard way as one day the media surrounded me and asked an innocent question. It simply was, "Why are you making a comeback?" and I confidently answered, "Because I feel I can still pitch better than half of the pitchers in the American League." The pitching coach was ready to attack me over the article that came out the very next morning quoting me saying that "I could pitch better than half of the pitchers on the A's." Wow, it took Dave Stewart and a couple of teammates to separate us.

Oh well, so much for getting off to a good start. This man obviously didn't care very much for me but it was okay, I had an experience with a couple of redneck coaches in the minors. I was very blessed to have Rene Lachemann as my very first manager in the minors, so I knew the difference. Coincidentally, he was the third base coach on that team, which was extremely comforting to know someone could co-sign for my character which was in doubt. There also were others that could vouch for me that knew what I was about. It was a humbling experience to no longer have that feeling of clarity and clout.

As the season started, I didn't make the starting rotation as all my appearances in spring training were starts. My competition for that fifth starter was Scott Sanderson who pulled a hamstring and missed a start or two, but to his credit, he sucked it up on his last start of the spring, went six strong innings, and was named the fifth starter. As I became the long reliever, I didn't have the type of arm that would allow me to pitch every day. So, it's up to you to play catch every day to keep your arm strong, and during batting practice before the game.

The pitching coach comes up to every reliever every day except me as to how your arms felt or give some sort of advice. Again, I didn't let that influence my performance, as I continued to work diligently and professionally. I was pitching well out of the bullpen in 27 innings I compiled a record of 1-0 with an even 300 ERA.

27.0	IP	Innings Pitched
24		Hits
10		Runs
9	ER	Earned Runs
0	HR	Home Runs
9	BB	Base on Balls (walks)
16	SO	Strike Outs
2	HBP	Hits by Pitch

It was All-Star break and on the way home on the
plane, I approached the pitching coach about a possible
start. We had a doubleheader to make up at home from a
previous rainout, again in hindsight, I used poor judgment.
He was enjoying a few beers when I asked him would it be
possible to get a start. He looked at me as if I had lost my
mind and without hesitation or the ability to care how I
might have taken it he bluntly said, "You're not good
enough to start on this staff." Wow, I don't think being shot
was as painful as those rude and calloused remarks that
were made! Realizing this was only going to get worse, I
returned to my seat still in shock as it hit me that no one
had ever told me, when it came to pitching, that I wasn't
good enough. Well, this story gets better... actually worse.

Upon my arrival to the stadium the next day, after batting practice, I was told to go upstairs and see the general
manager. Oh no, this can't be good. Well, I was right; I
had been sent down to AAA. I was put on waivers for just
$25,000, and no one picked me up again! This brought me
to the deduction that I was probably once again, blackballed.

I finished the season in AAA, where I went 0-1 with a
3.72 ERA in 3 games, 2 starts, 9.2 innings pitched. Why
wasn't I being pitched as the blackballing began again as
no one picked me up. The next season with no team signing me I gave it one more shot and played in A ball in the
California League with an independent co-op team in Reno
where I pulled a hamstring and was extremely ineffective.

The A's sent my first big league pitching coach, who is
a wonderful man to scout me, Wes Stock. It must have
been uncomfortable for him to watch me be a shell of myself, looking washed up and needing to retire. Then after
the game, he expressed my exact sentiments so that pretty
much solidified my decision to retire. I decided on the next

road trip, which was in San Jose, approximately 40 miles from my home in Oakland, that if I didn't throw to my expectations, I was going to call it quits. Regrettably, that day came, and I battled a young Toronto Blue Jays team that made me look and feel old as I pitched 5 1/3 innings trailing 4-2. I exited for the very last time of my incredulous career.

All good things must come to an end as it was a great journey filled with controversy and inquiry. This is not about revenge, just karma, what goes around comes around. In other words, when you do wrong it comes back at you.

"Vengeance is mine, says the Lord, I will repay." *Romans 12:19.*

This is why I've forgiven you (Major League Baseball). "And when ye stand praying, forgive, if ye have ought against any: that your Father also which is in heaven may forgive you your trespasses." *Mark 11:25-26*

In conclusion, I'm going to address the sinful nature of greed. It can make you do things that can be conceivable which can lead to things that have heavy consequences and are regrettable. Obviously, the organization viewed it as a fantastic business decision which was a remarkable payday of millions and paid me the bare minimum of $100,000, what a profit. After this type of exposure, was it worth it? You suspended me without pay in the sum of $900,000 in the last year of my contract. In hindsight, shouldn't that have been enough to retract? It appears you sought revenge. But I put it in the hands of the Heavenly Father and He will avenge.

"Yea, they are greedy dogs which can never have enough, and they are shepherds that cannot understand: they all look to their own way, every one for his gain, from his quarter." *Isaiah 56:11*

"Therefore I say unto you, what things so ever ye desire, when ye pray, believe that ye receive them, and ye shall have them." *Mark 11:24*

It shouldn't be very hard to guess what I'm praying for, Amen.

"It's not about your reputation, it's your character that matters."

"If you're not making mistakes, then you're not doing anything. I'm positive a doer makes mistakes." *John Wooden*

3. THE LEGACY OF BLACKS IN MAJOR LEAGUE BASEBALL

Back in the beginning of the Black baseball player's legacy in Major League Baseball, there was a man named Jackie Robinson. He was born in Cairo, Georgia in 1919 to a family of sharecroppers. His mother, Mallie Robinson, single-handedly raised Jackie and four other children. She moved to Pasadena, California where she raised them with heavy emphasis on spirituality and education. Those were the tools that gave him such a strong foundation. Little did he know that he was handpicked from Heaven to be the first Black to integrate MLB back in 1947. Physically he appeared to be terrestrial, but spiritually and mentally he was celestial. I'm proud to be a part of the great heritage and legacy and just as ashamed for blemishing his supremacy. I hope to be forgiven for not displaying at times, his type of decency. This is an attempt to make amends to the MLB, my family, fans, and friends.

There are no words to describe how much he's appreciated. Just like Martin Luther King Jr., he just can't be duplicated, as they're even more difficult to be emulated. They are the true definition of being emancipated. They are the epitome of man that represents a larger reality, a prime example of an immense amount of ability, responsibility and accountability in which basically constitutes stability. This is why on July 6, 1944 while enlisted in the U.S. Army, he refused to sit in the back of the bus and was court-martialed and tried. He was later to be found not guilty and declared he was within his rights. Little did he know that this was just the beginning of his many advantageous fights.

There was another incident while playing in the Negro League, when their bus made the usual stop for gas. Jackie needed to use the restroom. As the attendant was pumping the gas, he asked him if he could he use the bathroom. The attendant emphatically said no, Jackie immediately requested him to take the nozzle out and stop pumping the gas. After doing the math in his head quickly and deducting the loss of a considerable amount of money, reluctantly, the attendant had to say okay. This was another victory on Jackie's resume. From then on, that approach became leverage to everywhere they stopped and got gas. Now that's telling Jim Crow where to go. So you see just as much as he had to be passive, he was much more demonstrative in character, like massive.

The person Mr. Branch Rickey was looking for to be the first Black couldn't be just conventional. Oh no, he had to be providential. He couldn't be a racist nor an atheist, but quite the opposite, he had to be an antithesis. That's right, in order for Mr. Rickey's three-year plan to work, Jackie had to promise Mr. Rickey he wouldn't fight back regardless what was said or done. Mr. Rickey literally and purposely verbally abused Jackie prior to being signed to see if he would react. Of course, Jackie didn't and that's the reaction Mr. Rickey was hoping for so he wouldn't have to retract.

After that meeting, he wouldn't have to worry about that much anymore. He signed in 1946 with the Dodgers and was assigned to the Minor League Montreal Royals team. It must have seemed as if it was a dream. He clearly was the best player on the team. The next year, in 1947, he broke the color barrier winning Rookie of the Year in the National League. In 1949, he was the National League's MVP. Finally, he was inducted into the Hall of Fame in 1962 with a career batting average of 311, 96th of all times. They say behind every strong man is a strong woman—Mrs. Rachel Robinson. She once said, "I never heard

Jackie say he wanted to quit." As he was determined to succeed, so many more Blacks could have the same opportunity to make it.

Then came Larry Doby, who was signed with the Cleveland Indians. He was a centerfielder and was elected finally into the Hall of Fame in 1998. Perhaps no one is more remembered for being second than Larry Doby. He was the second African-American to play in the modern day era after Jackie Robinson. He was the second African- American manager of a major league club after Frank Robinson (also born in Oakland, California).

Major League Baseball began to explore through the Old Negro Leagues for many more. In the fifties, there were more Black players, such greats as Willie Mays (as a kid, he was my idol), Frank Robinson, and Hank Aaron. Aaron was amongst the last to come to the major leagues, as the Negro League slowly became barren. Willie, Frank, and Hank passed the baton to Ernie Banks, affectionately known as "Mr. Cub," who just recently passed away. If you met Ernie, you knew he was from up above. With his infamous quotes, "It's a beautiful day for a ballgame... Let's play two!" That's how much he loved the game and Ernie, the game loved you.

It didn't take long as it was quite clear that the best players in the game were Black. Well it appears America, through baseball, has taken a giant step forward and not back. For those owners who proclaimed they didn't want to integrate the game, they all had to eat Jim Crow as they needed to personally thank Mr. Rickey and yes, every single one of them should be embarrassed and ashamed! They are forgiven because racial ignorance is difficult to be explained, just look how long it's remained.

Then the sixties came, but now the players have different sounding last names. As then there began an influx of Latin players from South America, the Caribbean, and Central America. The newly found gold mines: Panamanians, Venezuelans, Puerto Ricans, Cubans and perhaps the best and most plentiful are the Dominicans. Names like: *Aparicio*, the first Venezuelan to be inducted into the Hall of Fame in 1984. *Oliva, Marichal, Clemente, Tiant,* and *Minoso* (who was the Latin Jackie Robinson of baseball). Minoso made his debut in 1949, and played 6 decades, the most in major league history. Why he didn't make the Hall of Fame is a mystery. In hindsight, what transpired is the Latins have basically replaced the Blacks and that's why with this knowledge I can't sit still. It's an injustice and for Black players, they are becoming the victims of a global economic ordeal. Within my eyesight this is very surreal. Potentially, this has the makings that Latin players are in popular demand. Was this the start of a machination, conspiracy, or a well thought out plan? Watching the predator attack its prey. Baseball is a glamorous lure motivated by pay!

Fast forward to today, the lack of Black players will leave you in dismay. The immensity of the Latin players has come without delay. As the sixties came about, Blacks finally gained their civil rights, behind the non-violent approach of the great Dr. Martin Luther King Junior's plight. As a result, Blacks are able to eat, drink and sleep with the rest of the team and stay at the same hotel. That prolific and victorious fight was that the Black ballplayer was able to excel. Now Blacks have become a preponderance, contributing to the economy while supporting their team and favorite player with their showing of strong attendance.

On the field, the Black players were second to none, watching them play made baseball appear to be much more exciting and fun. What a huge difference from what it used to be; opposed to the lonely Jackie Robinson, as he was basically just trying to blend in. Major League Baseball, let's not come to this again! We move forward towards the future, but in hindsight it already has. Who passed gas and didn't say excuse me? That's just not class.

Okay, that's enough humor, let's not regress, this next subject and person is all about the three S's: **S**weat + **S**acrifice = **S**uccess. Curt Flood, in my opinion, was the second most significant player to play the game. He is responsible for baseball's historical and controversial free agency.

Curt Flood was another Black pioneer. He sacrificed and jeopardized a brilliant career. Like all great leaders, they illustrate immense bravery and basically no fear. As he and the founder, Executive Director of Major League Baseball Players' Association Marvin Miller's prior experience was as an economist and labor leader. He combined those skills and the players' association became his creation. Together they battled and sued Major League Baseball with ferocity and no fear. This took place in 1966, as it turned out to be a monumental year. Curt never prospered from it financially because he was blackballed physically and literally. This is by no means a hyperbole. Their hard work and sacrifices are the reasons we have these incredulous salaries today. I think most would agree, that's safe to say. In my opinion, Curt should be remembered like Jackie is celebrated, in Oakland where he was born and reared. We started the Curt Flood Foundation as I was chosen honorary chairman, which made me quite proud and elated. How about retiring his number in a commemorative way as in he too, should have his very own day.

The 40's, 50's and 60's have passed and now we're heading into the 70's. Blacks are accumulating most all of baseball's prestigious awards, ranging from the Cy Young (best pitcher), All-Star selections, Gold Glove recipients (best fielder at each position), Rookie of the Year, Comeback Player of the Year, and MVP, which is the Most Valuable Player of the Year. After receiving any one of these awards, from my own experience and others, it can be very emotional to the point that it can make you shed a tear. How great is this accomplishment?

Frank Robinson is the only man in the history of Major League Baseball to be the MVP in both the National and the American Leagues (also from Oakland). He played for the Cincinnati Reds of the National League in 1961 and the Baltimore Orioles of the American League in 1966. The second one had to be the most difficult, due to the compounded mental and physical fatigue. The fact that he was just traded from the National League in '65, and in just one year to the American League in '66 he becomes MVP. That just added more intrigue. Black stars and the game of baseball are at a peak. Now when we walk, we don't squeak. Did you notice, I said we? I signed my very first professional contract in 1973. Two seasons later, I made history by becoming the 35th pitcher to throw a complete game shutout in my major league debut. Yes, that was like a dream come true!

Speaking of true, have you ever heard of the nickname *True Blue*? I had a teammate who was a pitcher and he threw so hard they named his fastball the "Blue Blazer." It was powerful and fast like a laser. I'd be willing to bet, that he could have thrown a ball through a car wash and it wouldn't have gotten wet. Here is another clue, he was the first pitcher to win MVP and the Cy Young Award in the same year. If you don't know by now, that is enough clues,

I'm through. His name is Vida Blue. We remain best of friends today and that's something I'm very proud to say!

I had another teammate who was also great. He was one of the greatest and most intimidating home run hitters in the game and is a household name. Finally, in New York, he received the well-deserved fame that produced a candy named the *Reggie! Bar*. Now I'd say that's significant, that's self-explanatory, it's who you are—a really big star. I'll even go as far as to say he's a superstar. After an illustrious career that spanned 21 seasons, with 1,702 RBI's, 563 home runs, 2,584 hits and a 262 batting average. He was voted a first ballot Hall of Famer. Better known as Reggie Jackson all over the world as one of the greatest to ever play the game. He respectfully earned the name "Mr. October." He outwardly hit home runs in the World Series, over and over and over. That's right, three in a row, now that's what I call putting on a show. It was like watching a baseball game that is a video, "The Destruction," a Reggie Jackson production.

Sorry, but I would be terribly remised if I didn't mention two of the previous greatest base stealers and record holders for steals, Lou Brock and Maury Wills. In 1962, Wills set a new Major League Baseball record with 104 stolen bases. In 1974, the 35 year-old Brock mounted a successful challenge to Maury Wills' 12 year-old stolen base record, amassing 118 steals while finishing second in the National League's Most Valuable Player voting. When you have class like these two gentlemen mentioned and when you get your record broken, it doesn't feel demoting. When you have class, such as they do, the correct and proper way to view it is as relinquishing. Yes, stealing bases can be very distinguishing.

Next came a whole new thing, his body looked like it was carved out of a rock. A powerful set of legs better known as wheels. As this young man proceeded and obsessed to break the record of Lou Brock. He accomplished this legitimately without the use of steroids or pills. To watch him play was the price of admission and it was definitely a thrill. He played with an incredible burning desire, while he ran as if his shoes were on fire. His name was synonymous with the Yankees' great "Mickey." He was simply known in both leagues as "Rickey." The first time I

 saw Rickey play was in spring training in 1979 as I was in need of pitching some extra innings. Therefore, they sent me down to pitch against the A Ball team. The competition was projected as less and it was, with the exception of one player who hit a long drive into the gap that bounced over a waist-high fence.

What came next was an innocent combination of comedy and suspense! Meanwhile, the runner kept running because by now he's in his home run trot. The umpire stopped him at second base with the discouraging news that it was just a ground rule double. Now the base runner had become emphatic trying to explain that it was indeed a home run. Finally, after being rejected, he was so passionate I thought he was slightly close to getting ejected. Now he's on second base and he takes a decent lead, I look him back once and then delivered the pitch to the plate. Simultaneously, he takes off towards third base. After a cloud of dirt and dust, the umpire, with excitement, even in his non-biased voice yelled "safe." When the game was over, I went to meet him and compliment him on his game.

I said he was the closest thing I've seen to Willie Mays. He played his first six years in Oakland wearing #35, so when he gets traded to New York it was an eye sore. He then changed to the legendary Willie Mays #24, coincidence?

I'd like to take the time to address my feelings about Mr. Henderson. We are aware of his physical talents that are extremely immense, but what you need to know is his greatest gift of commonsense. Rickey is the classic case of "what you see is what you get." There is nothing about him that suggests he operates under false pretense. In his rookie year, I chose to accommodate him by allowing him to become a roommate in my four story home. After reading this you'll have a better understanding and meaning of the word *fate*. He meant more to me than a teammate. You see, I met Rickey at a point in my life where I felt extremely irate. Life was trying to make me contemplate whether I wanted to continue a career that was in strife.

I was demoted from the major leagues to the Eastern League Class AA, after going 0-5 the previous year experiencing one of my two 20% cuts. Owner Charles O. Finley (whom I affectionately and facetiously called my White Daddy), felt I needed a wakeup call. He said I didn't appreciate enough being in the big leagues and that I needed demoting. Now I had to travel by bus and no longer the plane. He said, "I want you to go down there and smell some bus fumes for a while." Little did I know my career was on trial. To me it wasn't time to panic, that's just not my character neither my style. After arriving, I sat in my hotel room contemplating whether I was going to quit or was I going to stay. After being insubordinate for the eighth day, I decided this wasn't the right and neither the smartest way. Therefore, I swallowed my pride, got down on my knees, and attempted to pray. Thanks to the Heavenly Father I was hesitant, but I was on the field the next day.

When I was there, I was somewhat uncomfortable, like I was some kind of exhibit on display. In all actuality, I was to my dismay.

The mental uneasiness and anxiety led to my perturbation and consternation. That was the Heavenly Father's way through the solidification of His displeasure with me pertaining to the defamation of myself, through my act of insubordination. Then when it came time to pitch I was obviously terrible. After the game back home alone, Rickey wasn't that kid anymore, as he spoke like a man who was grown. He said to me, "You used to be great but now you're garbage." He said it very convincingly without hesitation or room for the imagination or misinterpretation. Well as they say "the truth hurts" and unless I fix this, it wasn't going away.

I got to the ballpark early the next day, to work extremely hard to prove my roommate wrong. I wanted him to eat his words, like a horse eats hay. It's now from my last horrific start on the fifth day and it was time to pitch again. I felt prepared from my diligent and somewhat excessive workouts since my last start. I shook off the cobwebs and pitched an outstanding ballgame. The very next day I was called back up to the big leagues. Mr. Finley expressed, "I just wanted to see if you were going to go down there and quit." Mr. Finley was extremely intelligent which included his incredible wit. He had such phrases as S+S=S (Sweat+Sacrifice=Success), which was my favorite. Also, "Pigs get to be fat hogs and go to the market." The last analogy is one I never quite understood in reference to contract negotiations. From my extended demotion, I learned a valuable lesson at the cost of mental fatigue. I had to get better, which made me approach the game with more passion and intrigue.

So in conclusion, thanks to Mr. Henderson for contributing to my prolonged, prosperous, and a pretty successful career. The attributes that I admired and acquired from him were how he played the game with enjoyment and passion, while playing with absolutely no fear. Here are some of his statistics that led to his Hall of Fame career: 297 home runs, a major league record of 81 lead-off home runs, 1,406 major league record of total stolen bases, 279 batting average, 1,115 runs batted in, 2,295 runs, and in 1990 he was the AL MVP.

The next individual I must say, with all due respect, and comically speaking, came close to being a murder suspect. I threw a pitch inside a bit too tight, which the 6' 5" 245 lb. physically intimidating and self-imposing man named Dave Winfield didn't anticipate. He most definitely didn't appreciate while falling rapidly and landing somewhat awkwardly to the ground. At that particular moment, my decision to pitch him inside didn't seem too sound. At this point he jumped up and headed towards the mound as I attempted to put on my meanest looking frown. All of a sudden my brave or crazy catcher from behind grabs the belt buckle in the back of his pants, maybe he shouldn't have done that. Mr. Winfield got even closer to me. It felt like David and Goliath and I also needed God to be *relieth* (a biblical word). Then he went into a slight rant, as he looked like a giant and I felt like an ant. He yelled out at me and said, "I should kick your little skinny ass." His eyes became big as baseballs, right then I knew this was a potential downfall. He turned around and looked at the catcher and said, "But I'm going to start with your ass first," while grabbing him by the throat and commenced to choking him to the point I thought he was going to suffocate. I guess he was letting us know that coming that close to his head was something he didn't quite appreciate! My catcher had the appearance of a rag doll being shaken from side to side. It was like being at Disneyland, I didn't want to get on that ride.

Although all joking aside, I was slightly terrified to see that type of strength Mr. Winfield displayed and utilized. After both benches cleared, that last pitch was ball four and he proceeded to go to first. I sincerely thanked God for not letting that escalate. This is a true depiction that I jest with levity; but to me after this was all said and done was a total comedy. No way am I attempting to tarnish Mr. Winfield's name or career. Let me tell you, this gentleman is class-personified on and off the field, as well as a person I totally revere. With that being said even though he was an opponent, he'll always be my peer. On the field, he was a *five-tool player.* A five-tool player is a player who has five different skill sets; running, throwing, fielding, hitting for average, and hitting for power. Most players have three tools, few have four, and even fewer have five. Here are some of the reasons why you get to play 22 seasons:

- He received 5 Gold Glove Awards in 10 seasons (compared to my 2 that I received in 1980 and 1981).
- He accumulated 3,100 hits, 465 home runs and knocked in 1,833 RBI's.
- He is the first 40 year-old to drive in 100 runs in a season.

Now that's what I call a gamer! That's how you eventually become a Hall of Famer.

My next great player is Tony Gwynn, better known as 5.5, but unfortunately is no longer alive. He died of cancer

in which he couldn't survive. The medical profession, suggests that his cause of death was due to chewing tobacco. To our youth, don't try a dip or some chew because this could possibly happen to you. So if you're trying to emulate your favorite pro, if a teammate or a friend offers you any form of tobacco—you just say no. Major League Baseball has banned the use of chewing tobacco, because the elongated use could possibly be your foe.

These are some of his amazing accomplishments on the field as he made most pitchers yield. There weren't very many balls that he hit were pop flies. That's how he got the nickname 5.5, hitting the ball between the third baseman and shortstop. Watching them unsuccessfully catch it after an attempted dive. He hit 300 or better in 19 of his 20 seasons. Why was he a first ballot Hall of Famer? Just like all Hall of Famers—he was another gamer. What consistency as he played in 15 All-Star games, that is an incredulous achievement.

Here is an example of the degree of difficulty to be selected to an All-Star team. Here is my soliloquy, I only made the All-Star team once in 10 years. I was also snubbed once, and was mysteriously left off the ballot by three writers for the prestigious Cy Young Award voting in the same year. My style was flamboyant or in baseball's terminology I was considered a *hotdog*. Regardless what was thought of me, I considered myself an anomaly, because I could perform exceptionally and successfully. I didn't mean to digress so I suggest we get back to Mr. Gywnn, who only won one Gold Glove Award but, out of all his accomplishments this one meant the most.

In conclusion, he was a humble superstar without the need to brag or boast. Here's to you Mr. Gywnn, you deserve this special toast because you, as a human being were the most, now you get to play for the Holy Ghost.

Now we're moving into the eighties and 19% of major leagues players are Black. It appears baseball, from a racial aspect, is headed down the right track. Statistically, the game is racially 73% White, 19% Black, 6% Latin, and 2% Asian. Man-up is defined to be brave or tough enough to deal with an unpleasant situation. The person I'm referring to is Baltimore Orioles' Adam Jones. He said, "Baseball is a White man's sport." There is a very large audience that supports his claim. This is proven visually, statistically, and now verbally! Every team has 4-5 brothers. Even better, Blacks have become millionaires and can afford homes for themselves and their mothers. It appears we're now able to communicate and associate more freely with one another. We started receiving guaranteed contracts with deferments and extensions, making it more fortified and stronger, which would enhance the player's security to play longer. Hold on, here's a deep scenario and the probability of a player living on the same block as your owner, or around the corner. Your new neighbors will still treat you like a foreigner. America, this addresses you too, and baseball fans as well. We all know the process it took to integrate the game, and it was hard as hell.

In 1947, Jackie Robinson showed that sports can have a profound societal impact. It seems odd to think that the sport that showcased Robinson is becoming inaccessible to many of the urban youth in the 21st century. Blacks have been heroes to American society, which has led to a decrease on the major and minor league rosters. Again, baseball has to take a different stance, because right now it has very bad posture. Did the owners come up with a fair and equitable solution? What they came up with stinks and it's caused some type of pollution. I've named it, "Operation Exclusion and Collusion."

In the late seventies, a regrettable and unfortunate turn of events came about when the drug cocaine entered the game. Preferences temporarily changed to amphetamines, which most players and myself found that type of speed was a little extreme.

In my rookie year on my major league debut, I got to my locker, and I discovered a blue pill. My naivety, and more so curiosity, wondered what it was for, because I wasn't ill. So I discreetly threw it away, as I had to worry about whoever left it and how they might feel. Being accepted and respected as a rookie is an extremely big deal. Three years later I finally tried one, and I pitched and lasted only 3 innings and I was done. It was my worst outing in my career and in conclusion that day wasn't what I considered very much fun. It was embarrassing as this is what I mean by extreme. I experienced hearing sound effects such as when the ball's rotation was spinning so fast, it left my hand and I could hear the seams. Then, hearing the ball with an explosion either hitting the bat or not too often the catcher's glove. After that horrific debacle, I promised I would never do that again to my Heavenly Father above.

Now cocaine was running rampant, it had gotten big, even Olympic. It was safe to say it was close to becoming an epidemic. This was so huge in the commissioner's eyes he had to take it to the FBI. Some players got reprimanded, some got apprehended, some got blackballed and me, myself and I almost didn't get to play again at all. To make an example, the FBI apprehended and imprisoned four players. Three of the four were Black and the other, perhaps for the sake of appearance, was the token White. The one superstar, or the big fish, was Black. He was sentenced to 90 days; he obviously was cut some very appreciative slack. Unfortunately, it's safe to say, the majority of the players sought out were Black. They were indulging in the "Miami Vice" lifestyle. In the ownership's eyes, we were looked upon as ignorant, disgusting, and vile. Yes, we had become offensive but never malicious or hostile. This was a new thing that the owners couldn't, but didn't want to, although had to comprehend. All's the owners wanted was the nightmare to simply end.

Are you ready to attempt to uncover Operation Exclusion and Collusion? Let's see if we can make it surface, and solve this confusion. We will accomplish this by getting rid of the misinterpretation and illusion. It starts in the grass roots, as baseball is like the forbidden fruit. It appears our Black youth apparently and preferably are playing football and basketball. It seems as if these sports have replaced our great game. To lose our fans and players because of racial bias would be a darn shame. The NFL has more Black quarterbacks due to the exposure of quarterback Doug Williams, who was the first Black quarterback to win a Super Bowl.

Then literally came a whole new thing; he as a basketball player turned out to win 5 championship rings. Better known as the "GOAT," the Greatest of All Times. I proudly present to you Mr. Michael Jordan as he literally flew through the air dunking basketballs and winning championships. This is what NFL and the NBA have in common; their leagues are predominately Black. That's simply why they have eye appealing and sustainable relationships. This gentrification is another machination in the disguise of

discrimination. This also is alarming in Black neighborhoods, due to gentrification their changing baseball fields
into soccer fields. To the Black communities, soccer has
absolutely no appeal. It has taken away a safe and fun
place to chill and perhaps enhance their skill. From out of
the parks and into the streets. It's just another segue setting our youth up for life's viciousness and cruel defeats.
Making them vulnerable and susceptible to rob, steal, or
even worse kill.

So now where do our youth go and what will they do?
Oh, by the way, incarceration is another machination too.
Being locked up behind bars is like being in a zoo. Your
parents, believe me, aren't happy nor proud when they
come to visit you.

This next little scenario is about when I attempted to fill
out an application to obtain the usage of a baseball field. In
order to do so it turned into a very uncomfortable and
somewhat of an embarrassing ordeal. The questions were
personal as well as insulting, such as inquiring how will you
spend your funding, that was totally unreal. This was very
strange and unusual, to the point that it felt surreal. As that
proved to be the deterrence in obtaining the field. To my
knowledge there aren't many, if any, scouts coming in the
neighborhoods and inner cities. That's part of the blame,
which has been the very pathway on how Blacks were
chosen to play the game. Now it's called advanced scouting, with the aid of computers and its newly found analytics. In my opinion, it's camouflaged and is another form of
discrimination, racism, and politics. Obviously, I'm biased
so I may not be a fair critique.

Analytics is the discovery and communication of mean-
ingful patterns in data. Here is a parenthetical quote from a
football head coach of the Buffalo Bills, "Analytics are used
as part of the preparation. They work better in baseball,

look at the tendencies. They are more advantageous in baseball such as righty against lefty pitching matchups."

Perhaps analytics are the new prerequisite for managerial positions as the Seattle Mariners took their general manager out of the front office and right onto the field as the manager. He replaced, at the time, the lone Black Manager Lloyd McClendon. He was fired and hired and has suffered a demotion down to the AAA Minor League affiliate Toledo Mud Hens of the Detroit Tigers. He has no qualms about stepping down from the majors to the minors. He said, "Hell, I'm a lifer." I hope he's being politically correct or he's a pretty darn good liar. I don't know which one it is, because it's hard to decipher.

Upon my first time hearing about analytics, I presumed it dealt with numbers calculated by an outside agency. I then wondered were there any Blacks holding these jobs? I'm almost certain there's no vacancy. That would only further solidify the conspiracy.

Now we're about to dig a little deeper. This information is the real keeper, after consuming this you won't be termed or considered a sleeper. Did you know all 30 major league teams have a baseball academy in the Dominican Republic? It's a thriving multi-million dollar business. MLB itself estimates that teams spend $125 million a year on the Dominican Republic Sports and Education Academy and an estimated $700 million in signing players. MLB, you must put some money back into the African-American communities. This is blatant discrimination. Owners, we must create a dialogue and much better communication because this is getting close to being labeled an abomination. The more the merrier for the Dominicans and less is best for African-Americans. It's simple math as former Colorado Rockies, Dick Balderson once explained, "Instead of 4 American guys at $25,000 each, you sign 20 Dominicans for $5,000 each." So you sign them at the ages of 15 and 16, after being fed a nutritional diet they gain about 20 pounds. Then at 18 they're headed to the United States with dreams of turning their lives around. In the academies, they play games against other teams in the league. They get instruction from qualified coaches with fundamentals daily. This is the criteria they must teach, as well as the learning of the English language in order to enhance their speech.

So is this a business decision or racism? My criticism makes me totally divided by my own cynicism. Let's not get this twisted. I'm happy for the continued progressive opportunities for the Dominicans. I'm just concerned how the Blacks are limited and afflicted.

Again, I feel MLB is the culprit and it was not until a former Detroit Tiger, long time minor leaguer and a product of Los Angeles, presented a proposal that expressed his concern of the rapid decline of Black players playing the game professionally. His name is John Young. He suggested that Major League Baseball become more attentive and I'm holding your feet to the fire by suggesting that you start being more anal-retentive.

The results from his proposal turned out to be Major League's RBI Program, which its initials stand for Replenishing Baseball in the Inner Cities. This is what confuses and angers me. If MLB spent $1 million per year in the 30 cities that they play in it could be used for developing talent and prosperity through educational enhancement in the African-American and other under-privileged communities. Obviously, our youth aren't a priority, politics victimize them, but that money could be spent on further educating them while learning valuable life skills and their lives where they have more of a chance to live it advantageously. Blacks are Americans, despite being called and viewed during the catastrophe from the hurricane Katrina as refugees.

It seems every so often, as a race, we get displaced. We know we're from Africa, but our roots can't be traced. All our heritage and history is as if it's been erased. This is why the past is my experience. The present is my responsibility, and the future is my challenge. This is the wisdom and truth I give our youth so they can maintain their balance. They need equilibrium, physically and mentally to achieve stability. Our youth deserve the opportunity to excel inside and outside their communities, with the ability to potentially enhance their skills in a structured and safe facility.

Yes, I'm aware of your RBI program, because I brought the first one to San Francisco. It turned out to be a total fiasco, which was a complete embarrassment. We had a 16 game schedule and were unable to get funding. I had to pay for the team out of my pocket, as I couldn't even afford uniforms. Out of the undeserving respect for that unwilling individual (he knows of whom I speak of) in the RBI program. I will spare you the rest of the embarrassing details on how it failed. To have a team, it requires a corporation to do funding and sponsoring. Trying to obtain it a lot of times is demoralizing, frustrating, humiliating, exasperating and sometimes downright degrading. You must swallow your pride because you feel as if you're begging. Although when you hear the basic universal phrase, "Sorry, but we can't help you at this time," which means a big fat disconcerting no. Whoa, another blow to the ego, it's not personal, it's just time to go! It's not what you know; it's who you know.

I speak from experience, and I continue to pray my program will take precedence. My program is called, the Mike Norris School of Baseball Health and Wellness. My motto is, "A Pitch to Success." My goals are to assist in cleaning up this mess, to help rid future generations of racial tensions, and to dispose of the unnecessary self-accompanying stress. Our youth, they are just children, they should be  treated special like you would treat an honored guest without duress. What happened to the quote, "The more, the merrier?" It doesn't say "the less." The game of baseball has rapidly been becoming antiquated; this terrible decline was not anticipated. Black parents, encourage your kids to play. If there is a baseball team around locally, sign them up today. Start them off at ages 6, 7, or 8 because 12 and 13 is a little late. This is why after 25 years of existence of the RBI program over a million kids participate, but less than ten have made it to the major leagues. Why? Until recently, the age group of the participants was 13-16. Again, that's a little too late. This is the age where there is an absence of fundamentals along with losing them to the streets. Due to the lack of mentoring and poor coaching, their lives soon become incomplete.

Then there is socioeconomics. It analyzes how societies progress, stagnate, or regress, because of their local, regional, or global economy. This is a significant disadvantage that most Black youths have come from a single parent. Most likely, it's the mother who can't replace the father. Who should be teaching their son how to hit, catch, and throw? Just being there, to provide and watch their son grow, is all that is asked. There is a ton of money in this game to be made, but first, we must take care of those grades. Now you have options if you're good enough to go to college or the pros and get paid. This is simply known as good old-fashioned bargaining power. When executed successfully, you and your whole family's lives can transform within an hour.

Every major league contract is guaranteed, even if you're injured permanently, or if you're in the last two years remaining on your contract and your performance turns sour. The key is to prepare for your retirement. This is what you must comprehend, that there will be a day when your career comes to an end! You must save your money, be an investor and prosper from your interest and dividends. The owners are now offering player's contracts in excess of 130 million dollars over ten years. In my era, (1975 to 1990), that was unheard of. The thought of a contract like that would have been ludicrous and entirely abstract.

When you make that type of money, you better know more than how to add and subtract. As the saying goes, "A fool and money will soon depart." It's apparent that this would be an act of negligence, irresponsibility, or just not being very smart. If you blow all that money, reality dictates that kind of money you can take care of your children, and your children's children, and so on. Think big, it doesn't have to be a fantasy, make it a reality and create your empire or dynasty.

Moving right along, because of steroids I chose to stop writing about them in the eighties. These are some Black players I've deemed to be steroid free, as there is no blemish to their integrity. Here are the names of these notable Hall of Famers and great ballplayers: Eddie Murray, Ozzie Smith, Frank Thomas, Ken Griffey Jr., Jim Rice, Kirby Puckett, Andre Dawson, Dusty Baker, Dave Stewart and Mike Norris. Yes, that's right, me. If only I could have stayed healthy. In my eyes and many others from 1980 to 1981, I was the best pitcher on the equator. On the field, I was a gladiator, as a teammate I was the motivator, and off the field, I was a celebrator. When it came to style, I was an innovator.

Finally, with all due respect, I'm going to turn my attention to the beast, whom I call facetiously but passionately, as it continues to move mysteriously. The beast has a title, and it's called "ownership." It's vastly starting to resemble a dealership. They buy and sell, also sounds a lot like slavery. They are all the same color except for one. How many Blacks? None! Historically, Blacks have been the means to Whites prosperity. More so out of fear, just another demeaning form of strategy. Having to be pragmatic in order not to cause static or then you'll become problematic. It's a group of roughly 30 incredibly wealthy individuals that own major league franchises and only they have a membership. This is about business, not a friendship. Until the basic agreement was administered, free agency owners literally and basically owned you. You had to play on a team without the right to be traded. Before agents came along, we were unaided. Negotiations were more like assassinations. They simply just annihilated, obliterated, and ultimately downright humiliated you. After it was all said and done, you were left feeling morbid.

BLACKBALLING—to vote against, to form a secret ballot, to exclude socially, or to ostracize. In baseball, I describe it as a form of collusion, where the owners agree to an unwritten effort to refrain a player from ever playing again. I personally can speak on this because it happened to me. I have a better one than that, how about me being blackballed twice? This topic is described in the chapter "Commissioner Peter Ueberroth, the Czar That Went Too Far." This chapter is written about merits and a variety of controversial and plausible events, such as the cocaine era and Steve Howe's seven documented and failed drug tests.

The league moved quickly and silently to eradicate a growing epidemic. As in this book, I tell what it took to get the league off the hook and Billy Martin's supposed excessive pitching of his historical staff. Did he ruin his starters' arms, mine included? Or, was it the strike-shortened season that was reduced and diluted, in which one contributed to my so-called demise? Guess what? I made it back to everyone's surprise. The Heavenly Father already predicted it through His forgiving and glorifying eyes.

I reported to spring training and little did I know I was working on borrowed time, resigning after being blackballed for four years. Now I'm in a quandary as it was brought to my attention that I needed to take a deposition. That wasn't explained to me prior to my acquisition. I wasn't in a good position to ask what's up, or why, so I figured I'd take the darn thing and shut up. Why did I have to take a deposition and for whose benefit was it for? Did this mean I was no longer blackballed? I was told the team's reasoning for resigning me was obviously I could still pitch, and I had paid my dues. That was an understatement. Out of all the lines he could have used, that's the one he chose to choose. Did the team display some moral compass, or was it the multi-million dollar insurance policy that they took out on me? Stay tuned and be on the lookout for the book currently being written about me coming soon. I will give you these heartfelt answers to the scenario, while I uncover the truth through the team's deception and greed. For this is the first time I have planted that seed. In the end, what matters is what I will be—substantial and consequential. It's my honest accusations opposed to the owners' reputations. The game has come a long way, but without the Black athletes playing the game, it's all at a standstill.

The game doesn't have the same look nor feel. It's no longer America's favorite pastime. Football and basketball are gainfully thriving, on the other hand, baseball appears to be nose-diving. It has lost most their Black fans along with its Black players. There used to be a handful of Black managers; now it's down to two; Dusty Baker and Dave Roberts. Except for Dusty Baker, Lloyd McClendon and Frank Robinson were the first. There is very little thirst, and it appears to be getting worse. What they all have in common is that they were managers in the big leagues more than once. Now with the usage of analytics, and without the knowledge of it, will you be considered somewhat of a dunce? In baseball, there has never been a Black owner. Mr. Moreno, being Latino, is the only one of color to own a Major League Baseball franchise. The team is named the California Angels. Then, there is Mr. Michael Jordan who is the only Black owner of a basketball franchise, the Charlotte Hornets of the NBA.

There are only three owners left from my era in which I played. I give extreme accolades to Mr. Jerry Riensdorf who receives a pass as he has tenure over the rest, in my book his experience and longevity makes him the best. He was second to hire a Black general manager, Kenny Williams, who had the fourth longest tenure of all general managers. The class personified Ted Turner. He was the first to hire Black General Manager Bill Lucas in 1976 until his death in 1979. Presently, there are no Black general managers after the firing of the lone Dave Stewart of the Diamondbacks. So, when it comes to front office jobs, and when it comes down to Blacks, they are taking a step back. Was the offering of his job sincere? What kind of fair analogy can you make in only one year? Getting fired only proves that you're still not wanted here, being uncomfortable with Blacks in this capacity is your fear. It's time to share your power and equivalency and make this your priority. One day in the front office we won't be such a minority.

It's coming; the gays are coming out of the closet. If you hired one, would you look at it as socially redeeming or a financial asset, or just merely a threat? Marijuana is about to be legalized, that's very perceptive that you have recognized things are coming to pass and these are facts of life that you must continue to realize. Making the adaption for usage, punishment has been reduced from suspension to a fine. Now that's progression and a very positive sign. So, you see, making it feasible for Blacks to play baseball should be the least of your worries. Is the picture I'm painting becoming more clear? Or is it still blurry? I've got a lot more paint, and I should use it because this is bigger than a trivial complaint. I've been known to change my mind when it's about the truth that I'm trying to find. What I've known for some time is that some wonderful men who are a part of management are truly outstanding human beings.

Take Ron Schueler, who succeeded Kenny Williams, of the Chicago White Sox. In this case, he is a very reputable, knowledgeable, and an overall good and decent man that I know personally. He is someone I owe for his help that only a privileged few are aware and know. When he was with Oakland, during my first stay in drug rehab, he stayed a couple of weeks working me out to make sure I didn't get out of shape so that I could get back to the show.

Then there is Walt Jocketty, formerly a General Manager of the Cincinnati Reds, and the former Minor League Director of the Oakland A's. I can't praise him enough; he is just the salt of the earth kind of guy. Thanks for treating me like a man and not someone that just got high.

Finally, is Billy Beane formerly the General Manager of

the Oakland A's. He is another wonderful human being, genuinely someone I enjoy talking to and seeing. If I'm in need of something, I don't have to go through anxiety, while contemplating will he be accommodating.

These men are products of future thinking and are the beneficiaries of past owners' mistakes. For those who deny their racism, they are pathological liars and fakes. For those owners that are open-minded to change and equality you deserve a break. I don't suggest that you can go kick rocks and go jump in the lake. Presently, the NBA and the NFL have hired female coaches. Also, they have hired an openly gay player in basketball (now retired) and football drafted a gay player. What does it matter? What should it matter if he can play? Although he would have to be great if you're not straight. Women deserve the same approach and not reproach, give them the job if they can coach.

The Oakland Raiders were the first to hire a female CEO, Amy Trask. It appears baseball is a long way from these accomplishments in what these other franchises have done. It's no coincidence that the NFL and the NBA are predominately Black and in baseball, there's a disparaging lack.

Now it doesn't take a rocket scientist to figure out why baseball is no longer number one. I can't and won't be hypocritical, so I must admit that I was extremely appreciative to get the opportunity to a second chance to return to the major leagues. What was accomplished by it all, is that I'm able to stand again tall. I have become more knowledgeable, and a better and stronger man from my rise and fall. That's because I finally listened to my Heavenly Father's beckoning call. Through Him, I found unattested strength and determination which helped remove the guilt, anger, and frustration. Through it all, I made it back to my original destination. There was a time in my life when my reputation was tarnished leaving me with the feeling that my life had been garnished. Now, I'm a better person through my re-creation, now I have self-gratification through my spiritual maturation. When I need my Heavenly Father, I call on Him with no hesitation and I never, ever need a reservation. Don't have guilt nor remorse, because you didn't contribute nor participate in this significant act of support. Provide and procure an avenue to secure possibilities for Black youth to play baseball.

Many people share my exact sentiments, specifically, Blacks, but for obvious reasons, the main one being getting fired or blackballed. Therefore, they choose not to express themselves. Although at the same time let's not stand around and act like this is an accident. Or is this an act of entitlement? Please don't insult my intelligence that this is a coincidence. This took too many different pieces and components to have transpired. It's a machination, a very well thought out plan or conspiracy for Blacks to become the victims of deficiency, in the game of baseball. By removing the desire, now the game is affected by what's been done three decades prior.

Major League Baseball, please let me reiterate, our goal is to make a better attempt to rectify Black youth playing baseball by having a proper, equal, and a better protocol. If not, the machination will succeed, and for the future of Blacks, it will become even more unattractive and a lot less of a desire. To solve this one, I must continue to dig much deeper to inquire. I feel like the game is losing its disparaging appeal. Home runs are down, and this time it can't be blamed on the lowering of the mound. Have they gotten rid of steroids? The temptation and the possibility of usage and repeated usage were world-renowned. It has been short of bizarre and curiously considered profound. Does the game miss those great Black home run hitters?

We haven't had one in over a decade, how bad does that sound? The hitting of at least two back to back seasons of at least 30 home runs, it can't be found.

Fans, haven't you found yourselves reminiscing about the electrifying base stealing of Rickey Henderson, baseball's leader in leadoff home runs? That's what I call excitement; the feeling of great pleasure and delight which is an enchantment. Is the game losing its fun? Let's not forget about Vince Coleman who also stole 100 bases in a season. They made base stealing a science; they did more than just run. Therefore, pitching is dominating like it currently stands. Again, it doesn't take a rocket scientist to figure this out, to comprehend and understand. Ownership! Together we can break these barriers. Bring back baseball in the urban areas. We are better allies than foes.

So that you know where I'm coming from, I'm into this from my head to my toes. Owners, let's face it, the answers and solutions are right up under your nose. My deduction is the solutions surely aren't the Black player's reduction. This is why the Heavenly Father is the only one that knows how this story goes. As for me, it's about my faith as I'm witnessing it in astonishment, as it continues to accelerate as it grows. Curt Flood's actions were extremely significant, but in my eyes what we're trying to accomplish is most definitely equivalent. Those players, Blacks and Whites, couldn't unite with the brother. I'm sure as they look back, some may have regret and others are truly upset. It's because they had to decide based on intimidation and fret. Let's not repeat the same mistake, so we don't have to experience that same awful feeling or ache. As I stated in urban slang, "It must have hurted to have felt deserted." Don't even try to come up with an alibi. Because after the smoke had cleared Curt lost his career, and so did I. The truth may never be acknowledged, but I am good just as long as I know why. Here's the difference between Curt and me, I've got nothing to lose and everything to gain. I am sure if he is with the Heavenly Father he no longer has to feel pain. I must illustrate endurance to sustain. It's no longer time for wasting time and stalling; it's my time and my calling. Now it all makes sense because I'm guided by His eminence and presence. He leads, guides, directs, protects, and heals. These are just some of His actions, which makes Him inconceivably great, along with His tremendous and multi-faceted abilities and skills.

 Getting back to our youth, a couple of years ago our nation was under captivation. The annually televised Little League World Series brought us an immense amount of satisfaction, pride, and elation. We could see Mo'ne Davis, a Black female prodigy and incredulous sensation. Yes, I said a female pitcher, but if you had to bat against her, you couldn't tell. She made history by making the cover of Sports Illustrated to sell. For her many accomplishments, she should be congratulated and celebrated. Major League Baseball has inducted her jersey into the Hall of Fame. She is so well rounded, with good looks, brilliance, athletic, and very modest. She has integrity, appears to be straight-forward and honest. Wow! All the accolades and fame came from playing this wonderful game.

Here is another great story that's similar, but not the same. We move from an individual to a team. As this had the makings of their best dream. This is another story about God's magnificent glory. Check this out, how ironic is it that the name of this team was named after the first

Black man to play baseball in the major leagues and exceeded well beyond being famous, he was iconic. You are correct if Jackie Robinson was your guess.

An all-Black team from the notorious murder capital of the nation, the Southside of Chicago. They won the Little League Baseball World Series Championship. They were awesome as they accomplished their goal with speed, power, pitching, defense, intellectually, style, joy, and great sportsmanship. Actually, they were a PSA, or even more so, an unpaid commercial for Major League Baseball. It was some great and free advertisement. We were privy to witness God's special assignment. Surely, it wasn't a mere coincidence because it does have spiritual significance and resemblance.

Baseball has political and international connections with long arms. For example, possessing the abilities to consume assets through financial power, without the need or usage of charm. This sets off another very disturbing alarm. There may not be another Mo'ne, but I'm sure she inspired many more girls to play.

President Obama's restoration of full communications with Cuba has opened the door for Cuba's biggest financial exportation involving the Cuban baseball player. Now the only problem lies in the hands of the major league franchises, who don't know who gets the money for the purchase of the Cuban baseball player. Is it the government or the Federation of Cuban Baseball?

Presently we have a new commissioner of baseball, which personally, I'm glad to see this change. He's in support of countries that are influenced by baseball, which will expand the game's range. Will this present a similar opportunity like in the Dominican Republic where all 30 major league franchises have been monopolized to obtain exclusive rights and possession to gain control? Let's evaluate and unfold what needs to be told. In Los Angeles, for the last 26 years, the Dodgers have been involved in Major League Baseball's RBI Program per NBC, Los Angeles. "Dodger RBI is built on the belief that making baseball accessible to inner city youth can make a difference on and off the field, at school, in the community and in these youngsters' futures," said Dodger owner Magic Johnson.

The question is, do programs like MLB's RBI work? Dodgers, I would like to think this is about your moral compass, or is it the recognition and the perks? MLB's RBI programs have been around for nearly 30 years, but the number of African-American players in the major leagues has steadily dropped every decade since the 1970's. However, Major League Baseball–now a 9 billion dollar industry–has yet to figure out how to market the game against the other options a young Black inner-city male has. First, if your intent was for Black men to play baseball, then go where they live—Inglewood and Compton. In 2013, the Dodgers finally expanded their RBI program to Pico Union, Long Beach, and Compton after the organization's foundation commissioned a study that found those communities were underserved. Please, don't insult my intelligence, now do you see how one can get so frustrated and perturbed? Did they need a commissioned study to find that out; we're getting closer to finding out what this is exactly about.

Last year, MLB also created a diversity task force. It said it was to address the talent pipeline that impacts the representation and development of diverse players on the field personnel in Major League Baseball, particularly African-Americans. For that to happen, those in the highest ranks of the game will need to put actions behind those words. This committee consists of 18 owners, executives and coaches who have no physical presence in the specifically Black communities and can do no more than stick together like a flock of birds. You must hire reputable people from the ghettos. Perhaps starting at schools, playgrounds, and churches and gather them up like herds, not to appear like a bunch of nerds. This must stop, you're a necessity, but this calls for a league-wide cultural revival. That means hiring a new fan base which could be hip hop. Not only is it about providing resources where Drake or Snoop Dog can be in a television ad with Curtis Granderson, then MLB has some phone calls to make. How much money would it take? A lot less than what they spend in the Dominican Republic for Heaven's sake. We must also remember that young athletes desire heroes to extol, and for Black youths, there are only 69 to look up to in a league of 862 opening-day players.

This must have to do with economics slightly more than racism and race. Let's face it, this is means to an end. The truth is something you can't defend. Is exploitation a sin, because that's what's taking place in the Dominican. All the while, this has a beginning but no end! Money breeds success, and being Black, is that a race or color? For example, in North America, the term Black people is not necessarily an indicator of skin color or ethnic origin. It is more of a socially based racial classification related to being African-American, with a family history associated with institutionalized slavery. When will the color of my face not be looked upon in the aspect of race? Will our Black faces ever be associated with success? Yes, for the future of our youth, let that desire be their quest! Teach them pride and equality so they may acquire that taste. It's something that they can't replace, nor erase. Establish strong roots, those that can be documented and traced. Since our ancestors left Africa, we as a race, have been misplaced. After you sign a player he now has become a financial investment. More often, that could potentially turn into an uncomfortable or a non-profitable predicament. You've been down this road before. That's why going back down it again has made you somewhat hesitant and resistant. The reality of it is that it's a full-termed contractual commitment. Since this didn't work out before, there appears to be a form of stereotyping and racial profiling. This in turn leads to some slight resentment. So, what's the solution, when we can't receive a deserved restitution?

Our communities suffer from so much deviation of the norms of social behavior, which in a way is regarded as bad as in dysfunction. This comes from a lack of education, which brings upon provocation and that originates from a lack of communication. Education can provide a second career; it will alleviate after baseball is over standing on the corner smoking marijuana and begging for money for a beer! So, to counteract these results, if a player goes in the first five rounds, give him a full ride to college. If he goes higher, give him a contract with obtainable incentives to go towards college. This will improve his quality of life through the consumption of knowledge and will cause a transformation into a complete person and to restore the needed rejuvenation. This is a suggestion that would bring perhaps some connection to make a correction. I propose in every major league city, to use my criteria for an academy. This is the way you strengthen communities. Advocating education, nutrition, mentoring, and most importantly spirituality, to address social skills to eradicate dysfunctional behavior, such as truancy, bullying, gangs, drugs, alcohol, vandalism, and profanity. This will solidify and reward good behavior such as respect, hygiene, dedication, sportsmanship, and leadership. We encourage entrepreneurship, the process of designing, having, and running new business relationships. Exposing them to poetry, fine artistry, photography, performing arts, martial arts, aerobics, computer training, clothing designing, hair cosmetology, and charm and etiquette school. These are some examples of our after-school program curriculum and other tools. So, our youth can stop being the victims and become victors.

It's time for change as our 44th President has done a fantastic job. He has dealt with great complexity and extreme controversy. This gives me a lot of social redeeming value, as this is very inspirational and the fuel to finish my goal. It was a simple concept when I pitched, to finish what you start. Displaying the fortitude of having the combination of guts and heart. That was my forte, going nine innings, enjoying the thrill and satisfaction of a complete game! Although there's nothing on this earth that can duplicate that feeling, that will never be or feel the same.

What the legacy of the Black ballplayers has endured and accomplished is invaluable. They should be respected and admired even if it isn't required. Why? Because this great country of ours has prospered socially, historically, and economically from their diligent performances on and off the field. A goal for the near future should be to have sole Black ownership of a Major League Baseball franchise. Through hard work and sacrifice, that's a probability that sounds mighty nice. Comically and truthfully speaking, to purchase a team, he or she would have to be a world-renowned reputable celebrity. Billionaires coming with an impeccable background to meet their price. It's plausible to ask, will the Mike Norris School of Baseball Health and Wellness produce such a person? The game and ownership needs to welcome this type of diversion, because it's exhausting making all these aspersions.

In conclusion, I would like to address the African-Americans in the game. The game of baseball is no longer the same. You are the minority being suppressed by a majority. With that being said, more than ever before we now have the capabilities and with that should come responsibilities. Those being to give back to your respected communities. That would be as sweet as honey if you give your precious time and money. To help a build a church playground or a school would be cool!

Thank you and God Bless. I intended for this to be enlightening, not frightening.

4. BEING BLACK

Although the residual of slavery has led to our present state of degradation, being Black, you must deal with the immense humiliation. Don't internalize the situation; it only turns into an overwhelming frustration. Politically and economically, Blacks must become more aware.

It starts in your community, and comes from your participation, which shows how much you care. In order for you to succeed, you must have an education. There isn't much more that can make a parent prouder than to be able to attend your high school graduation.

It doesn't stop there, as college should be your next ambition. After receiving your degree, you're ready for life's heavy competition. Everyone can't be a rapper or play professional sports. I know this may sound discouraging and hard to conceive, but the odds of making it statistically makes it almost impossible to achieve!

The point I want to make is there are more significant careers or professions in order to succeed. More educators, administrators, doctors, politicians, and lawyers are what we need. Instead of being employees, it is time to start thinking bigger and become entrepreneurs and employers.

Separate and distinguish yourselves from procrastinators and destroyers. Blacks have come too far, literally, from being slaves and submissive, to becoming nonchalant and permissive, even to the point of being dismissive. As a result, Blacks have become extremely apprehensive. Blacks must become more intensive, which requires you to be more assertive, aggressive, and ultimately more progressive.

You must attempt and exercise this with an immense amount of concentration and dedication. Most importantly you must eliminate any resemblance of procrastination. After obtaining all these qualities, it would be virtually impossible to face incarceration. In your mind, jail should be thought of as an abomination.

Speaking of jail, I'm going to share something mind-blowing with you. After reading this information, you'll be shocked and amazed too.

The focus of this article is on the claim that the music industry executives invest in private prisons and promote gangsta rap music to influence young people into a life of crime. Thus, resulting in higher incarceration rates and increased profits for the investors. In other words, they obviously brag and boast, sipping on the finest champagne and making a toast. They wait patiently for another sister, brother or a significant other. I'm going to leave you with these references, so you can uncover the truth, as I'll present to you some proof. So maybe you'll get this knowledge to be able to uncover the reality that you will be able to discover. If you need more convincing, the following information will wake you up. It will revive you more than that morning cup of coffee or tea.

The media has so much power and influence, glorifying lifestyles of immortality that depicts the affluent or about affluence. Sadly, as unbelievable as it may be, sicker things have happened which were once labeled "conspiracy theories" until the supporting evidence was uncovered and documented. Ridiculing conspiracy theories may be popular amongst self-righteous contrarians, but their mockeries ring hollow in the face of the following real life documented government conspiracies. [1]

In the 70's, a movie titled *Super Fly* hit the screen. It appeared to have it all with its glitter and deceiving gleam. In reality, we haven't overcome that look of how many lives have and are being destroyed over a dream on a movie screen.

Super Fly was a lie, driving the nicest car, living in the best apartment, having the finest White woman and all the cocaine he could snort. As in the end, he and his Black woman pulled a cold game on the mafia and crooked cops and got out of the game with all their money and to top it off *Super Fly* put a hit out on the mob boss and told him, "If one strand of my pretty hair is touched, you're a dead man."

Young Black men, there is death in the streets and there is no such thing as fair out there. Times are too hard in life; you just can't exist if you walk around as if you don't care.

Blacks have come a long way from being slaves as you see the way *Super Fly* was portrayed, enticing images and illegal characters were to be a set up to be betrayed. That is only in the movies, to live happily ever after if you could. It only happens in Hollywood. But the residual of it was crack cocaine and the African-American community has never been the same. It's useless trying to find theories and trying to find someone or something to blame.

Amazing how drugs can destroy a community and a neighborhood; it's a crying shame. It will eventually disgrace you and tarnish your family's good name and your fame! This is why you need to show some interest in your

1. "Commercial Rap: A Pipeline to Prison?" *Rap Rehab*. N.p., 27 May 2016. Web. 02 May 2017.

African-American history, although most Blacks remain perfunctory.

Currently, political Blacks have excelled in the White House from the first Black Supreme Court Justice Thurgood Marshall to the current Black Supreme Court Justice Clarence Thomas. Condoleezza Rice the first woman to become Secretary of State. The first Black Attorney General Eric Holder who preceded the current Attorney General and the first female and Black Attorney General Loretta Lynch. The two of them were appointed by the most powerful man in the world, the one and only first Black and the 44th President of the United States, Barack Obama. These are some of God's great blessings as they are totally anointed!

Blacks are capable of being successful great leaders. In Africa, they were Kings and Queens. When the strongest survived that inhumane treatment on the way to America, the slave owners separated the remaining existing families. They used the strongest male and female sexually to do what is known as *breeding*. So more than likely the odds would indicate the child would be big and strong, better known as a *Mandingo*. In today's society, it still exists.

In our African-American communities, there are women who have babies just to obtain a welfare check. These women are known as *welfare breeders*. This should be a crime, because they are birthing innocent life into potential criminals. From the lack of a family structure, that child is literally a "born loser." It's not coincidental or subliminal to turn out to be a criminal. It's a lack of parenting; even at its best, it is minimal. Parents, you must become more resolute so you can become whole that's to constitute. You must address your family's actions and dysfunctions. You also must seek wellness; it is a major segue in conjunction. Be that proud parent to the point where you've shaped and molded your child and he/she turns out to be a savant. That's a person who demonstrates profound and prodigious capabilities. An example: Stevie Wonder is a musical *savant*.

Another dysfunction that needs to be addressed is teenage dating violence and just overall domestic violence. Black men, behind every successful man is a strong woman. Be superior but don't treat her inferior. Make her your queen, an equal, get engaged and marriage should be the sequel. Don't treat your woman with misogynous, respect her trust in you by making a strong effort to be monogamous.

Over 30% of African-American women are physically abused. [2] That's no way to treat a woman, leaving her afterward feeling frightened, insecure, embarrassed, beaten, bruised and confused. Black women, one way to resolve this is to call the police, press charges, and out of your life have him removed.

Until then, you can't expect things to improve. Through the grace of God, there are teenage and domestic violence programs; one I highly recommend is mentioned below. You must deal with this issue, don't take it lightly or somewhat pretend. If you're a family, seek counseling so you'll have awareness and then the ultimate goal is prevention. This is how you achieve wellness, it's redemption. Spare your child or children of these awful traits in becoming irate to infuriated and exasperated. You must seek help, there's absolutely nothing to debate.

So, to eliminate the confusion here is my conclusion, silence is not the cure for teen or domestic violence. I'm in partnership with an organization that is one of Oakland's

2. USDOJ, OJP, "Extent, Nature, and Consequences of Intimate Partner Violence: Findings from the National Violence Against Women Survey". 2000

crown jewels called "A Safe Place." It addresses issues such as:

24 Hour Crisis Line
Children's Program
Community Counseling
Emergency Shelter
Support Groups
Teen Violence Prevention

The mission of "A Safe Place" is to provide victims of domestic violence and their children with safe shelter and support resources. It also provides a community and education focused on reducing domestic violence. The following goals are presented:

1. Decrease the number of battered victims and their children becoming homeless or returning to the same relationship.

2. Reduce domestic violence in the community by providing community education and outreach to teens and adults.

3. Assist victims in regaining self-esteem and personal power.

"A Safe Place" takes a holistic approach in meeting their mission, focusing on direct services and prevention.

For more information on "A Safe Place"

P.O. Box 23006
Oakland, California 94623-0006
Phone: (510) 986-8600
Fax: (510) 986-8606
Email: asp@pacbell.net
Website: www.asafeplacedvs.org

Executive Director Carolyn Russell works tirelessly eradicating this epidemic.

Don't wait to seek help before it's too late. A happily ever after ending would be great! So, the moral of this story should be the answer to all things; put God first so you can receive His glory. Black parents, family members, and friends, this overall dysfunction must end. The time is now for that change to begin. Again, since this information is so extensive, I've put it in the form of a poem to make it more enjoyable and comprehensive. Basically, Blacks are underachieving in society extensively and here is the hardcore proof statistically.

Whites outnumber Blacks at 66% to 12% in the population of the United States. According to the most recent FBI statistics, in 2011 there were 2,695 murders in which the victims were Black, 91% were committed by the same race.

There are 14.82 murders per 100,000 by Blacks, versus 2.17 per 100,000 for Whites. Dropout rates: Blacks 8.7, Whites 2.3. Graduation: There is a misconception that half of African-Americans don't graduate, among the half not graduating with the cohort 5.8% get a G.E.D. which leaves us with 20% completion, 12% of Black males are graduating late. They can account for 38% of the 53% who are graduating with their cohorts; the remaining 15% is likely due to random error in including students transferring to schools outside their district.

So, you do the numbers, and see that Blacks are killing each other, going to prison, addicted to drugs and becoming alcoholics, with poor health/diabetes, high blood pressure, HIV/AIDS and experiencing domestic violence. All this is going on in our communities, basically with utter silence.

"Those who challenge the system will meet with great resistance," Jesse Jackson stated.

If that's the case, this will take immense endurance, stamina, and relentless persistence. As a race, Blacks must promote young Black male achievement. It's a necessity in order to procure, so Blacks can endure into the future. Blacks, male and female, must unite on the same accord with a mutual agreement. Education should be your common goal, it's what you need. It will strengthen your relationship and help you to succeed. Keep God first, and get that education, consume healthy food and drinks, and get a good female, preferably an educated and caring female, and stay out of jail!

So now you have concepts and a strategy as this is the way to stay out of a major catastrophe. There's no room for losers, copouts, and quitters if you're famous. Your nightmare has just begun, welcome to Facebook and Twitter. If you stay on the right path, you're on the way to heaven versus hell. You just can't quit; it's not an option. Look at all the great individuals who sacrificed and gave their lives for you. Before you leave this earth, you've got a lot to do! Jesus Christ, Martin Luther King Jr., your heritage, and all those African slaves. Have you done anything that they would be proud of? A couple of things they all had in common are that they were extremely brave and could give unconditional love. I can hear James Brown from beyond his grave singing, "Say it loud, I'm Black and I'm proud!"

5. COMMISSIONER PETER UEBERROTH, THE CZAR THAT WENT TOO FAR

Peter Ueberroth appeared highly successful and just as motivated, perhaps even more so innovative. My question is, did that thirst, tenacity, and drive ultimately expose his needs which were to satisfy his obsession with fame and greed? He's somewhat of a savant as a businessman and executive, but let me give you another interesting perspective. I'm going to flip the script and have him characterized, because what I came to realize left me totally mesmerized.

I'm going to start by calling the commissioner narcissistic as well as being egotistic. I'll even go as far to say he's a person of self-righteous indignation. It's my opinion from a bias but a valid observation. From the Bible, *Romans 10:23*, "For they being ignorant of God's righteousness, and going about to establish their own righteousness, have not submitted themselves unto the righteousness of God." Also, from *Romans 1:22*, "Professing themselves to be wise, they become fools."

For example, he testified in Washington before the House Select Committee on Narcotics and Control. In essence, he asked government officials to declare war on those "bringing the poison into our country," *L.A. Times*. During a lengthy interview with the *L.A. Times* was Ueberroth's tough talking on the topic which had little to do with him as the baseball commissioner and everything to do with him, Peter Ueberroth, self-imposed visionary, a three-piece suit rebel with a cause. "I'm kind of waiting for somebody to tell me I shouldn't be doing this," he said. "A few people in baseball said it's kind of inappropriate that my position doesn't really dictate that I do this, and I guess I have a hard time arguing with that." He continued, "If there was such a thing in the government as a czar of drug fighting in this country, and somebody asked me to do that, I'd be hard pressed to say no."

Ueberroth's interpretation of his and baseball's victory over drugs is taking action against it, in meeting the enemy face to face. To his way of thinking he came, he saw, and he conquered. This to me means I was totally dominated by the suggestions and commands of someone else! All this man needed was to legitimize himself with something consisting of some socially redeeming value. Some say his intentions were to become the newest non-politician who seemed to have his eye on the top job. Obviously, he wasn't aware that under the Reagan administration, the Iran-Contra and Nicaragua war of which was being funded by the CIA, was responsible for the firearms and drugs, which contributed to the crack cocaine epidemic. It was designed to destroy Black lives through death and incarceration. As it's known, Blacks are victimized as the users, and it's quite clear Blacks definitely aren't the producers.

Thirty years later Blacks gather to get this message that Black lives matter, specifically to our government agencies with their contingencies and conspiracies, all the way down to our local police and their eagerly awaiting correctional facilities. (read my poem, Chapter 12, "Cocaine and Its Delusional Pain" in detail) I explain. So, when Mr. Ueberroth made the statement, "The government must make the war on drugs a priority as urgent as combating terrorists in Libya and elsewhere." We're losing the war on drugs, and it's tearing the country apart. In 1986 there was a dramatic increase in the strength of narcotics smuggled into the country and a sharp decline in street prices which meant before long we may be way beyond the chance to win. I'm hoping that I'm painting a clearer picture of why he's called the "Czar." Heck, he pretty much spoke the words right out of his mouth. I suppose you are what you are, that's why I say he went too far!

Ueberroth challenged Congress to elevate the nation's fight against drugs to the fervor of the fight against terrorism. "If we declare war on Tripoli when the hell are we going to declare war on the terrorists bringing the poison into our country? We seem to risk everything to stop these (Libyan) terrorists, but we seem to be unable to stop the terrorists who manufacture the drugs and the terrorists who sell the drugs." "I'm angry, I'm scared, and I'm committed to helping this country declare war on cocaine and marijuana. It's over," he added, "You're not going to hear about any baseball scandals from this day forward." Ueberroth said of his year-old crackdown on drug use in baseball. Urinalysis tests for the 3,000 minor league players and front office personnel in the majors and the minors, has reduced drug use among prospective big leaguers from "unsatisfactory to infinitesimal." However, when pressed to provide documentation for his assertions, the commissioner refused.

Mr. Ueberroth, by today's standards in this country statistically, your efforts were monumental, but not that successful. It would have been interesting, challenging, and cool to witness you fighting that political cesspool. Throughout our nation, crack cocaine, heroin, methamphetamine, and marijuana are readily available and extremely profitable! They have the appearance that this can go on forever. While marijuana is America's number one cash crop and endeavor, it's probably the same government agency that's legalizing marijuana in our nation for profit, that you went to, to try and stop it. Even Major League Baseball has softened their posture, as the punitive actions are simply fines. That fits the crime, as I thought that to be pretty clever. Time brings about change, that's why you should never ever say never.

Racism, here comes the beast, the one that's so hard to beat and defeat. No longer do I have to cast these ugly assertions or unwillingly retreat. Now I have some proof and the truth...remain in your seats, fasten your seatbelts, this roller coaster ride is going to be a knowledgeable presentation of the deceit. I was left totally uncomfortable with the predetermined outcome of the disparity in numeration of Black players opposed to the number of White players that weren't named in this machination. This is a plan and goal for Blacks as a process of elimination and degradation. Deservedly so, I'm personally angered and insulted as these White players were basically given some sort of special anonymity. It wouldn't influence their future prosperity. On the other hand, the Black players are incriminated, degraded, and closely short of literally being annihilated. This is equivalent to being disabled, and being emphatically labeled. In my case, it was botched and fabled. This too will be explained later as this mystery that's full of drama will unfold as I reveal what's untold. In conclusion, the players that weren't named should also be ashamed, as they sit back and bask enjoying all the perks and adulation of their should be supposed and defamed names, some are even in the Hall of Fame.

Suspended or blackballed, who makes that call? Who will take the fall? It's 1985, my contract is over after signing it for the duration of five years. No one has signed me, yet is this possibly the end of my career? This has the makings of becoming extremely severe! Will my contemporaries still have revere?

The San Jose Bees became the place for us baseball refugees, which was an independent co-op team in the Class A California League. This opportunity didn't present itself with much intrigue. Perhaps what made it tolerable was the fact that I was only forty miles from my home in Oakland. As it turned out, it was a great place to land. The sole purpose of being there wasn't so much to enhance, nope, this was the place of last chance. Baseball has fallen out of love as it pertains to me, they have lost their romance. So, little did I know, due to an allegation (is an accusation in which is sometimes true and sometimes not) in law, an allegation (also called adduction) is a claim of a fact by a party in a pleading, charge, or defense. Until they can be proven, allegations remain merely assertions (again, I'll explain as the mystery unfolds as to why these allegations were made).

Time to play ball, on my team was a cast of four so-called misfits; myself, Ken Reitz (my friend and homeboy from San Francisco) also, Daryl Sconiers, and the most significant one, Steve Howe. There were others on the team, quite frankly, who weren't quite good enough, but just didn't want to quit with the exception of two, whose names were Steve McCatty and Jerry White. McCatty was my teammate and starter on Billy Martin's record-breaking pitching staff in Oakland that broke and demolished the major league complete games record. They were the only two big leaguers that weren't there for drug transgressions. They were just there to be picked up, to finish their professions. Although little did Jerry know about the creation of the machination (which affects older players as well, without guaranteed contracts). You see, that was the reason why he was there. Little did he know, as of a year ago at age 33, was to be his last year. His character is second to none, as to this day he has never done drugs and I don't ever recall him ever having a beer. How do I know this? Because ironically we grew up in the same housing projects. He being a couple of years older as we went to different high schools. As a senior, he hit over 500 and was the greatest ballplayer in the city of San Francisco, besides Joe DiMaggio, as the Montreal Expos drafted and signed him.

After returning home in the off season, he and several other minor leaguers, including Dick Tidrow and Dennis Eckersley, played on that team. It was well coached and managed by the Zuardos, the son being Lou, who was also the catcher. He helped very much in my learning process and the father, Vince, who I loved like my father as I affectionately and respectfully called him Uncle Vince. One day on the bench during the game I asked Jerry how was his season, he replied it was okay. After listening to his tone and looking at his facial expression, I asked what happened? He said they didn't start me. Being shocked and somewhat appalled, I said, "What?" in total dismay. He said they had some pretty good guys. Now I wanted to know who could be better than him? He answered, "Dawson, Cromartie, and Valentine." (LOL) After being out of the game for 12 years, the Minnesota Twins signed him in 1998 as their first base coach, as he endured it for 17 years. That's what I call a transitional success! Looking back, out of all of us, he was basically the only success story out of all of the rest. Again, stay tuned for more. Sorry not to digress, but this next individual is a person of extreme interest. After or upon mentioning his name you would most likely say, "Wow!"

Steve Howe had incredible individuality, a wonderful presence, and personality. When we met, it amazed me as we had a lot of similarities. He had immense capabilities and physicality. He was also quite the charmer; that was another one of his many abilities, as he asked my mother to cook him a home-cooked soul food meal, but he wasn't around to receive it due to his off-the-field accessibility.

Possessing a 95-mph fastball, being a lefty with a nasty slider, and while pitching, he had such a calm demeanor. Unfortunately, I only got to see him pitch once, and then he disappeared for four days as he was trying to get clean. It takes three days for cocaine to leave your system and the very last molecules to break down are called metabolites. They can show up on a drug test as a false-positive. Ironically, and allegedly, it was reported that the Toronto Blue Jays had come to sign him, but of course, Steve wasn't there, and for us misfits trying to get back to the show, this was a negative! Here is Steve's drug bio in a short narrative: He played for the Dodgers, Twins, Rangers, and the Yankees. He also played with two independent teams and twice in Mexico. This is the last and only place to go. He missed the rest of the entire season in '86 but was brought back in '87 by the Rangers. After '87 with the Rangers, he was out the next three years entirely. He received a lifetime ban from Fay Vincent in 1992, after pleading guilty to a charge of cocaine possession in Montana, but an arbitrator overturned the ban. Then his career was resurrected by the Yankees, and he pitched six seasons before he was released in '96. He was suspended a record of seven times while allegedly failing as many drug tests.

Drugs and tragedy don't discriminate, to be pre-destined with doom was to be his fate. God bless his soul as he lays in peace, as that demon, Satan, contributed to his decease. It was reported that on the way home from a business trip he fell asleep at the wheel at 6:00 a.m. and was partially ejected from his truck and tragically died. Toxicologists found methamphetamine in his system when he died. Methamphetamine is a highly addictive stimulant, chemically related to amphetamine.

Harry Steve is one person I must commend because I consider him my guardian angel and friend. He was the owner of the team in San Jose, and he saved my career from ending abruptly. One day I was feeling sorry for myself and didn't show up for the game. After agonizing all night, contemplating on retiring, I showed up at the park the next day. Surely, certainly, positively and definitely, when I showed up to the game the next day I was expecting to be released. Upon arriving, I immediately apologized and expressed to him my confusion whether I wanted to even continue to play anymore. Harry looked me in the eyes and asked, "Do you want to play if so you can play, who am I to end your career?" I'll never forget those words, as they came straight from his mouth, out of his heart and straight to my ears, as it felt so sincere. I thanked him and expressed to him how he just solidified and justified my reason for being there.

Well, to make a long story short, out of the four misfits Kenny Reitz and I survived and endured the entire season. I went 4-3 with a .154, in my attempt to get back to the big leagues and that should have been an enough reason. Again, no phone calls. Maybe I need to obtain a new agent as my previous one didn't pan out so well. He left my finances in a condition comparable to hell. So, desperate times bring on desperate measures. I hired Steve Howe's agent as my agent thinking if he got Steve several jobs then he must be good. I prayed this wouldn't be another accident. Well, I considered him to be very good and efficient, but it also didn't work out. He was cool; we never had an incident, he was quite sufficient. His diligent work consisted of lots of letters and phone calls, but I didn't get any response at all.

Major League Baseball doesn't perform or act according to regulation. It has been guilty of such matters as collusion, racism, and discrimination. This isn't hyperbole nor a fabrication; it is a terrible and horrible realization. The

Black ballplayer is full of expectations with very little gratification, that's just my interpretation. Permanent humiliation and elimination are the design for the destruction due to the machination. Let's not be naive, there are roughly 750 major leaguers each year and they only named 24 players (LOL), don't insult my intelligence and my due diligence. Believe me, when I say this, there were a lot more players that escaped the wrath and are now just masqueraders. Instead, the Black players are being appropriated, excoriated, and now are considered perpetrators, while not given the equal opportunity in the work place to be elevated. Have we been made out to be guilty of being both suspicious and egregious? This has become very arduous. Yes, some of us were made examples of, myself as well, and we were wrong as hell.

As for me, that covered both matters contractually and spiritually. The commissioner chose to put more emphasis on persecuting and prosecuting than what was more significant, such as saving a life in reference to rehabilitation. Alcoholics and addicts are a part of society, as well as baseball and the key to living a prosperous and healthy life is sobriety. We're just people that are medically diagnosed as having a disease. What else can explain literally blowing their careers and lives? Sometimes it's having to hit rock bottom and being totally demoralized and left devastated. Losing jobs, custody of your children and finally the divorcing of your wife, this is now your life, no more comfort just strife. This becomes the outcome if this individual is in denial and if he doesn't get help he'll continue running because drugs and alcohol are baffling and cunning. That only 46% of people who attended residential drug treatment stay in recovery [3] and the lack of resources for people when they're most vulnerable makes no sense. No doctor would help a patient control his blood sugar or blood pressure once, and then wave good-bye. The same should be true of addiction; it's a chronic disease that requires long-term, possibly lifetime care. So why is the care so scarce? "People go away for a month; it's supposed to be magical, but it's not. The successful transition of patients from inpatient to outpatient is abysmal," said Ray Tamasi, president and chief executive of Gosnold on Cape Cod, an addiction treatment organization. ☐

On February 29, 1986, Commissioner Peter Ueberroth ordered the suspensions of eleven drug users. They were categorized into three groups. I obviously fit into group three for whom testing was required encompasses those about whom less evidence exists regarding drug use or those whose cases have already been resolved. Seven were suspended for a year, four were Black, two were Hispanic, and one was White. Four went into a federal penitentiary for ninety days, of those, three were Black, and one was White. Four were given sixty day suspensions, three were Black, and one was White. Four others all previously acknowledged cocaine use and most were treated for addiction, three were Black, and one was White. Isn't this ironic that these numbers are similar to today's incarceration rates in our nation's prison systems? This isn't just a coincidence; this goes on every day!

From the ages of 17–25, one out of three Blacks will be incarcerated. Now, this is how I read in Mr. Ueberroth's report, as the fifth player (I was the fifth player on the list of eleven). "Mike Norris, a pitcher now out of the major leagues, might fall into that group," Mr. Ueberroth said, "after a criminal charge of drug possession in California is resolved." The charges were dropped, and the court ordered me to go to a thirty-day rehab, which should have

3. & 4. Rosenberg, Tina. "Staying Sober After Treatment Ends." The New York Times. The New York Times, 09 Feb. 2016. Web. 10 Apr. 2017.

sufficed for group three. Group three didn't require a suspension, although I was out of baseball, banned or more
like blackballed from the winter of '85 until my return in the
spring of '89. I personally am also aware that some of the
games' biggest stars, being Black, were obviously targeted
opposed to the few Whites which totaled a whopping number of three and none of them were starters. See how well
thought out this was to calling this what it is, a conspiracy?
Almost forty years later, this information is available for
everyone to see, for it has given me great clarity. Little did
Mr. Ueberroth know that he would be entering the era of
the internet and he literally got caught in the net.

In the winter of '86, I was summoned to meet with Mr.
Ueberroth in New York, but instead I met with a couple of
his officials. I remember vividly being highly upset after
leaving his office because they flew me literally clear
across the country to ask me two questions. These questions were, "Do you do drugs and when was the last time
you did them?" What was most insulting was he didn't take
the time to personally meet with me. I also remember
thinking that I must not be in too much trouble, but my curiosity led my antennas to go up as this was too subtle.
Were they making use of a clever and indirect method to
achieve something? It's very unlikely that it's just nothing!
The machination has started as the players are methodi-
cally being made to depart. I went to the player's association, but that was to no avail as they were no help as far as
I could tell. I even sought the most powerful Black advo-
cate in existence, the great Reverend Jesse Jackson. But
even he couldn't prevail. It doesn't take a rocket scientist to
tell that this has a smell, and not only me with all due respect, even Stevie Wonder could see. However, based on
the unions in previous cases, there was a strong possibility
that it would challenge the commissioner's decision

through baseball's grievance procedure.

Mr. Ueberroth, with the assistance of the owners, also facilitated collusion between the owner's violation of the league's collective bargaining agreement with the players. Players entering free agency in the 1985, 1986, and 1987 off seasons were with few exceptions, and prevented from both signing equitable contracts and joining the teams of their choice during this period. The roots of collusion lay in Ueberroth's first owner's meeting as commissioner, when he called the owners "damned dumb" for being willing to lose money to win a World Series. Later, he told general managers, that it was "not smart" to sign long-term contracts. Former MLB Player's Association President Marvin Miller later described this as a "tantamount" to fixing, not just games, but entire pennant races, including post-season series.

The MLBPA, under Miller's successor, Don Fehr, filed collusion charges and won each case. This resulted in a "second look" for free agents and over 280 million dollars in fines. Fay Vincent, who followed as Ueberroth's successor in the commissioner's office, laid the crippling labor problems of the early 1990's (including the 1994-95 strike) directly at the feet of Ueberroth, and the owner's collusion, holding that the collusion years constituted theft from the players. ☐

Mr. U., which one are you? My confusion is, are you political or hypocritical? You most definitely weren't hospitable, which is defined as friendly and welcoming to strangers or guests, or having an environment where plants, animals, or people can live or grow easily. As you literally came in and stole the show! The collusion also prevented me from filing for free agency, which cost me a

5. Interview – Fay Vincent – Former Commissioner Archived July 13, 2007, at the Wayback Machine.. Bizofbaseball.com (2005-11-09). Retrieved on 2017-4-10

whole lot of money. From '86-'88 I was out of baseball, or should I say blackballed! This contributed to another Black vacancy, is there any legitimacy? Now that should be considered, what you did through collaboration was grand larceny. You never had your feet held to the fire, of course I'm preaching to the choir. It appears you received some sort of pardon by being either let off or let up on. In the end, you went out like you came in, like a thief in the night. Mr. Ueberroth, I would like you to acknowledge *Luke 8:17* "For there is nothing hidden that will not be disclosed, and nothing concealed that will not be known or brought out into the open." In other words, what you do in the dark comes out in the light. Just remember, Mr. U., you started this plight, except you didn't anticipate a fight. You made it personal instead of initially, finding out who should have been deemed wrong, correct it, and get it right. Instead, your actions appeared to have been done more calculated and out of spite. Intelligent as you are, that wasn't very bright, as you eventually blew the goal of the presidential seat that was rumored you had in sight.

Of his term as commissioner, baseball writer Daniel Okrent noted in *Sports Illustrated:* "To a job previously occupied by the ineffectual (Bowie Kuhn) the invisible (General William Eckert) the incomprehensible (Happy Chandler), Ueberroth brought an authority effectiveness and public visibility that method those of Judge Kenesaw Landis, the man whom the job was invented in 1920."

Landis perpetuated the color line and prolonged the segregation of organized baseball. His successor, Happy Chandler, said for twenty-four years Judge Landis wouldn't let a Black man play. I had the records, and I read them and for twenty-four years Landis constantly blocked any attempts to put Blacks and Whites together on a big league field. Bill Veeck claimed Landis prevented him from purchasing the Phillies when Landis learned of Veeck's plan to integrate the team. The signing of the first Black player came less than a year after Landis' death on Chandler's watch and was engineered by one of Landis' old nemeses, Branch Rickey. Eleven weeks after Robinson's debut with the Brooklyn Dodgers, Veeck became the first American League owner to break the color line.

There is no doubt, that between the comparisons and similarities, that Landis and Ueberroth shared, it's almost uncanny! With Landis, it appears without Blacks, it was fine and dandy. The reduction of Blacks started on Ueberroth's watch from 1984-1987. As the numbers dropped in drastic proportions after his term was up, it was quite obvious who was head of the machination primarily against Blacks. Surely there is a connection to the collusion of 1985-1987 as the club's revenue increased significantly. Ueberroth denied knowing the collusion had taken place, but many believed it was part of the game plan for profitability. I feel personally that Mr. Ueberroth was originally and specifically hired to get MLB out of their financial instability. His powers and personal vendetta against the war on drugs super-exceeded all of his accomplishments as commissioner, which finally led to his misery. I can't call you a closer nor a finisher as it turns out your claim to fame is being a dispenser—his role as protector of the weak and dispenser of justice, but it's "just us."

Apparently, in an article in the baseball almanac there is a biography written about all six of the commissioners, and Mr. Ueberroth is one of them. I found some rather interesting quotes about him. This one is from Lee MacPhail in *My Nine Innings* (1989), "It is unfortunate that he did not seem to have the deep attachment to the game itself that would have motivated him to stay on. It is probable that he never envisioned his role in baseball as more than a temporary one." This article is about the commissioner's office in general. I suggest you take a moment, review each biography, and learn more about the men who actually had been called the "second most powerful men in America." Wow, baseball and politics are a replica to America.

Peter Ueberroth is extremely wealthy. In 1995, six years after he left the office of commissioner, he and an investment group made an effort to buy the controlling interest of the California Angels. It appears Faye Vincent and the tightly knit owners learned from his and their mistake, being aware of their reputations and status, what was at stake! We've seen over recent years, some great men fall, some leaving us shocked and appalled.

His inclusion would have affected you all. These actions you took also prevented me from filing for free agency because from the winter of '85-'88, I was blackballed out of baseball, which led to another vacancy, indirectly but purposely! Was that your strategy? Is there any legitimacy? However, and whatever the outcome was, I potentially lost a whole lot of income—meaning money. Reprehensible, deplorable, dishonorable, discreditable, despicable, inexcusable, objectionable, indefensible, and almost unforgivable, yes that's how I feel about you! Mr. U., for you to have taken the actions you took, you obviously felt the same way about us too.

Racism again, is still the motivation for causing degradation. Just the simple fact of what's inevitable, the disparity in numbers. There's not one White player of notoriety mentioned, especially the ones who have Hall of Fame credentials. Systematically, out of roughly 650 major league players, you calculated and chose an estimated twenty-four players mathematically. Mr. U., couldn't you have been a little more diplomatic and not so emphatic? Couldn't you have shown a bit of mercy or even given us amnesty? You became judge and jury and we became the brunt of your fury. We were basically forced into surrender while some of us didn't even have as much as a public defender. Cocaine had become an epidemic and the use of it had become easily accessible and academic. Isn't that why you brought in the FBI? There were so many players that were indulging, if you did the mathematics, you would have probably need a counting apparatus!

I've intentionally chosen to not use any of the Black players' names simply because part of conspiracy has dual implications, by becoming labeled through public embarrassment. This can possibly stay upon you forever, with the possibility of ruining future employment or other endeavors. Again, I would like to reiterate that I'm not crying over the milk I spilled, please believe I have enough remorse for straying off the course. I've accepted my transgressions and basic immaturity, but that's how I found out that I have more mental than physical dexterities. I'm simply coming from a place of wanting to be treated fair and square as a civilian, and not a villain. What I've grown to know is they can't condemn me even when they conspire.

Behold the Heavenly Father "for the Lord your God goes with you; he will never leave you nor forsake you." *Deuteronomy 13:5*

"So that we may boldly say, the Lord is my helper, and I will not fear what man shall do unto me." *Hebrews 13:6*

Well Mr. U., I can't honestly or exactly say I enjoyed doing business with you, but the Heavenly Father fixed what was misconstrued. Facetiously speaking, I sure hope you didn't feel as if you were being abused. I think you have better clarity as to why I entitled this chapter, "The

Czar That Went Too Far." Your resemblance was more of a senator or a governor, than a commissioner. Although I'll give you credit for cleaning up the cocaine from the game in which that you're due, but if I knew what I know now about Major League Baseball, I'd sue you. It's been forty years and it's not about the money, it's about this machination and I've gotten down to the core. The journey I took was over rough physical terrain but as usual it's the mental aspect that propels your brain. This is what you have in store after being knocked down, it picks you back up off the floor without you even feeling sore.

The truth has removed the unknown, no longer having to accept my life as a partial failure or simply blown. From all of this I've aged, thus being alive and as a man I have wisely grown. I no longer have to be imprisoned with guilt after being dethroned. The Heavenly Father has avenged this, and when this is all said and done, I'll be back on the throne. I think it's safe to say we all learned a valuable lesson between right and wrong. As a result, I've become increasingly and considerably strong!

In conclusion, we're basically not monsters, dumb, stupid, immoral, or unacceptable. Although without the resources and knowledge to get well, our actions or appearance can appear to be deplorable. While to most alcoholics and addicts, sobriety almost seems impossible. For me, my Heavenly Father is whom I give the praise and the glory, all the while giving him the credit because He's a transition not a transaction like a debit. As for He, and only He, is responsible, dependable and the best thing is, He's affordable! Why, because you don't need money, He can take all the dark clouds, such as drinking and drugs, and make your day feel bright and sunny.

When you stop smoking, drinking and drugging, you'll have some extra money. I'm as serious as death, and I don't find this to be very funny. He intervened on my grave and I became saved, and therefore I've been illuminated and raised. That's why He's worthy to be praised. Through the Father I chose His healing; it was much more appealing. From all this newly found exposure, I've finally gotten some closure. Then in the words of the great Dr. Martin Luther King Jr., you can shout out "Free at last, free at last, thank God Almighty I'm free at last!" Through the Heavenly Father smoking, drinking, and drugging can be a thing of the past and can be removed from your life extremely fast. Why wait, don't hesitate, there's nothing to debate. It's your life, you must participate, or you'll spend the rest of your life full of regret and hate. Believe me, you have better things to do with your time than to contemplate.

Put the power back in your life, to regain the ability to negate. Then you'll eventually resist the urge to perpetrate. You too will be able to relate, when you surrender through time, you'll obtain tenure. Then, let the Heavenly Father relate, not dictate, but delegate, freeing up your mind so you can concentrate and then you can emancipate.

6. WHY AREN'T BLACKS PLAYING BASEBALL ANYMORE?

The Heavenly Father has given me a platform,
So, that I can describe and better inform.
That what I must talk about is somewhat out of the norm,
I'm setting off the alarm.
We're going to talk about something other than my right arm,
I'm not trying to display my charm.
Only to expose what's going on,
And I don't fear any bodily harm.
And if you're a racist, after reading this you won't feel very warm.
This is for all demographics,
Whether you live in a mansion, condo, the projects or on a farm.
I just sadly think of Jackie Robinson and what it took for him to perform.
A man with so much talent, pride, and dignity,
But to succeed he had to be humble and conform.
Why aren't Blacks playing baseball today?
After reading my book, you'll be able to tell if there's foul play.
Does it have to do with the cocaine era that quietly went away?
Major League Baseball, in my opinion, started its machination.
Blacks being the culprits, through the act of elimination,
While the little league level is victimized by gentrification,
To me, it's a form of discrimination.
Last year there were only seventy-three Blacks on opening day rosters,
Major League Baseball, it's time to take a different but fa-

miliar posture.
It's best for the game, and everyone can prosper,
I don't want to appear to make this improper.
I just want to bring out some denial and awareness.
Through my experiences, this is what I must offer,
There's no way to make this softer.
They say the truth hurts,
Well, from holding all this in,
I'm about to burst.
Not taking this to my grave
Driven there in a hearse.
But this boils down to economics and politics.
Now they have a new gamesmanship,
It's called analytics.
Just another form of discrimination, those jobs go to the Ivy
League schools of higher education,
Where is the media? Someone must bring greater expo-
sure to this situation.
They're changing baseball fields into soccer fields,
Is it plausible the parks and rec and city hall are making
deals?
There are still the same two fields where I played on in my
community,
But again, it's politics and economics as the Catholic
school girls' softball is a priority.
So, this is an enticing segue into gang life and street dwell-
ing,
To make some money, it's drugs they're selling.
Unfortunately, the average Black single parent family can't
afford for their child to play the game,
Blacks are being forced out economically, and that's a
shame!
It costs $100 to $300 for an aluminum bat,
What's up with that?

$100 to $500 for a glove,
Now that would come from a lot of prayer to the Father above!
Turf shoes or spikes, it all depends on what he likes.
They cost $60 to $150
Are you uncomfortable mom?
He's growing up,
It's time to get him a jock strap and a cup!
Batting gloves cost 20 to 80 dollars
That just covers the equipment.
To play on a travel ball team is as much as 1,000 dollars, to be able to pay for that would be a heck of a lot of sacrifices and a major accomplishment!
Afterwards, this is enough to make you want to holler,
All because of the lack of the almighty dollar.
So, there you have it in short form,
Again, the Heavenly Father gave me this platform to inform.
With this being said, the compilation of these facts and figures is a clear depiction,
Why Blacks aren't playing baseball and this ain't no fiction.
As I speak from a concerned and sober mind with immense and sound conviction,
I can't go to battle alone.
I need people with guts or money,
If you have both, then we have growth,
If we're going to change these cloudy days back into sunny!

7. BILLY MARTIN, THE MAVERICK

The Maverick, but you didn't know the man was also a Christian. The man that had class, and no matter what city we were in on Sunday, he would be at 6:30 mass. He was an apologist, strategist, as well as a psychiatrist, a father figure and a true leader of men. I even felt close enough to him to consider him as a friend. The *N.Y. Times* described Billy as being celebrated for his ability to motivate players but was notorious for fighting with them and others. Perhaps Billy got that honesty from his sweet and just-as-tough mother. Being short in stature and a name such as Alfred, yes that's right, his real name is Alfred Manuel Martin. He was born on May 16th, 1928 in Berkeley, California in a diverse community. Bill Pennington wrote a book about Billy entitled "Baseball's Flawed Genius." Some players perceived him to be heinous, odious, atrocious, and even monstrous. His genius included the brilliance of the coined and phrased "Billyball" as well as Kool and the Gang's hit song, *Celebration*, which immediately played after each win. Very few fans left early, most fans stayed to the very end. Billyball was created through his brilliance, as we played tough and fundamentally sound baseball with great detail and resilience.

Before Billy's arrival in Oakland, he had been the N.Y. Yankees' manager, as he had a love-hate affair with his boss and said owner, who Billy once referred to as a convicted liar. George Steinbrenner fired Billy five different times. By the way, with all due respect, the way Mr. Steinbrenner treated Billy was a crime. Oh well, as the saying goes, "One man's trash is another man's treasure." Coming to Oakland was going to be a pleasure.

Billy was somewhat unorthodox as his thinking and actions were totally outside the box. He was idiosyncratic, a distinctive individual with individualistic characteristics. He was ahead of his time as he used statistics to create advantages, defensively and offensively, to put us in favorable or superior positions against our opposition. As we fast forward to today, the game's usage of statistics has a name called *analytics*. Just another aspect and illustration of his genius while managing us, and quieting his critics.

Spring training 1980, on the very first day before we even took the field I had already gotten one foot in Billy's doghouse. In a meeting, as we gathered sitting in our lockers, Billy began to explain what was expected of us. Then he began to explain how some players screw the coaches and managers, as he then concluded, "If you screw me I screw back harder!" As I observed the utter silence, and the fear that struck most, it became so comical to me, I almost bit a hole in my lip attempting not to laugh, which was unsuccessful. Then it seemed to become even more quiet, more like distressful. In somewhat of a look of disbelief, he angrily told me to meet him in his office after the meeting.

Now I'm praying we don't get into a fight because my thoughts were it wouldn't have been me taking a beating. I knocked on his door as he abruptly answered come in, I came in, and he said to close the door and sit down. I sat down and he immediately asked me what was so funny. I replied, "Well sir, after you said if you get screwed then you'd screw back harder, the fear that you imposed upon the rest of the team was comical." He then asked why wasn't I scared and I replied right off the top of my head without hesitation, "I don't plan on screwing you, sir." It must have been a great answer because he had this look again on his face of disbelief. Then all at once he gathered his composure and said, "Okay, good enough now get your ass out there on the field!" I left his office thanking

God for giving me enough sense to yield. That day turned out to be monumental as it had all the makings of being quite detrimental, as I became trustworthy, respectable, reputable, eventually even estimable and honorable to him.

What about my talent? Billy saw me pitch against his Yankees the year before Thurman Munson's death due to a plane crash. It's my first time in the newly renovated, iconic Yankee Stadium. On this night, it was abnormally subdued, not the usual mayhem or even the disruptiveness of bedlam. Not even the traditional boos. I pitched into the seventh inning, and I felt I was very competitive. I vividly remember pitching against the great Thurman Munson as he proceeded to go three for three against me. All three hits were perfectly placed through the infield, while one of them hugged the third-base line for a double as all three hits he got were on fastballs. What I didn't recognize was that the first hit was a chopper up the middle, the second was a ground ball base hit between third and shortstop. The last one he was totally sitting on a fastball as each at bat got the head out quicker. After his second hit he stood at first base, stared at me, and shook his head, so I thought he was trying to get into my head. His next turn at bat my inexperience and ego got the best of me as I tried to throw it harder instead of slower. Again, he sharply hit it down the third base line as it bounced off the stands in short left field in that oddly configured ballpark for a double. Now, he stands at second base as if I had insulted him. I'm so angry as I looked at his face, all I could see was the short stiff hairs of stubble. He yelled at me, "You got to be the dumbest S.O.B. throwing me all fastballs!" After that, my slogan became, "To make progress you must learn to acquire finesse." So, where was I deficient? Let's start with the changing of speeds, pitching inside and hitting my spots with more consistency with velocity and great location. Billy watched me from the very top dugout step with an intimidating observation. I suppose I passed his calculated evaluation as he processed and stored the necessary information. Little did he, and neither would I, know three years later that I'd be the ace of the staff in his starting rotation.

The dry spitter, Art Fowler, Billy's friend, confidant, and revered pitching coach, whom I also loved, tried to teach me the dry spitter and a pitch called the *sailor*. In today's game, it's known as a *cutter*. The controversial spitball is an illegal pitch because you put a foreign substance on the ball, which can vary from Vaseline to your own spit. This pitch is thrown with velocity with the appearance of a fastball but sinking drastically downward like a sinker breaking perhaps as much as two feet. It made it virtually impossible to hit. Well, the dry spitter didn't work well enough as far as consistency, so that was it for me.

My first spring training my catcher, Jeff Newman, (whom I nick-named Nu Nu), and I had an epiphany. This took place after I got two strikes on the hitter and as usual, Nu Nu looked into the dugout to get the sign as to what pitch to throw. Little did I know, the next pitch would be an anomaly.

Going back to my first professional season in Class A, I threw in the mid-nineties with a rainbow curve and a 90-mph screwball. The timing of the arrival of roving pitching coach Bill Posedell had uncanny accuracy. Before my first start he saw me throw a bullpen session, throwing the ball hard as I could trying to make a good impression. Then he asked me to throw some breaking balls, I proceeded to throw a couple of good curveballs.

I'm feeling pretty good about my performance so far, now it's time to take it up a notch. I threw my screwball that went roughly 90-mph, and Mr. Posedell said, "Stop, I've seen enough," as he had the look on his face as if he saw a ghost. "You're not going to hurt that arm, not on my watch." After I threw, he and Manager Rene Lachemann made the decision for me to stop throwing the screwball. What was uncanny timing is that this happened before my first start. Again, thanks go to my Heavenly Father as He always does His most significant part.

ANOMALY- something that deviates from what is standard, normal or expected. It's the definition of the screwball with my exact personality described perfectly. Will this upcoming two strike pitch improve my career im-mensely? Let's see how this evolves, pay attention and watch intently, as my career is about to become into a frui-tion successfully. This pitch now has no limit or amount. It can be thrown in at any time in the count. This perhaps is the most intriguing aspect of this soliloquy. As I left you waiting as to what happened, when Billy chose to call for the dry spitter. Nu Nu and I had a secret that Billy didn't quite know about. That is when on two strikes I had an op-tion. Instead of the dry spitter I would throw the screwball and get a strikeout or a ground ball out. Wow, it's already paying off through Billy's guidance and firm leadership, now I've just learned some gamesmanship. I finished with six strikeouts in four innings and an inning ending double play, I say that was quite a successful day. To this date, Billy never knew that I was throwing the screwball instead of the dry spitter.

From that day on I left suspicious American League hitters angry, frustrated, and bitter trying to hit that illegal (in their minds) spitter. I sought a psychological advantage over the hitters by going further into the game, and watching the opposing team become quiet, and then subsequent quitters. Now hitters are looking for where I'm supposedly hiding the Vaseline, therefore, not being fully able to concentrate. They proceeded to step out of the batter's box and call a timeout to ask for the ball as I fully cooperated. It was always clean, leaving them extremely frustrated. I often wondered if Billy had ever found out the truth that would have left a bad taste in his mouth, possibly a little sour or even bitter. I honestly don't believe he would be embittered, or would he have smiled? In his case I think a smile would have been a frown turned upside down.

I'm continuing to work hard and pitch well the rest of the spring training. My goal was to first make the team, and if I didn't make the starting rotation I wouldn't have been complaining. I had accomplished both goals. Not only did I make the team but I was named the fifth starter. Now I'm feeling good about myself as my confidence was back, knowing that I had greatly improved and had become much smarter.

It's my first start and it was a masterpiece like classical art; only giving up 1 unearned run, 11 strikeouts, 1 walk, and scattered 3 hits. In getting my first win, uncontrollably across my face came a well-deserved grin. As I went on to go 5-0 with a 0.36 ERA, with 41 strikeouts in 50 innings, before losing to the Blue Jays 1-0 in 10 innings. After this particular game, to say I was angry would have been an understatement. It felt like it took an eternity before I became an abatement. Little did I know that my anger made quite a statement. I took a baseball bat into the bathroom and proceeded to beat the toilets, sinks, and anything else in my view, until I was through. I finally came out five to ten minutes later; some of the team might have viewed it as unwarranted, except Billy. Him having an appreciation for my elongated performance was all I wanted. He had this look on his face between adulation, appreciation, and admiration. Billy then looked at me and said in front of the whole team, "Michael Norris, you're the ace of my staff." That took some guts on his behalf. What a change of emotions for me, turning from mad to sad to heck of glad. I just experienced my first loss of the season, and my newly found disdain for losing. Was Billy rubbing off on me, is this the reason?

Well, I guess I couldn't leave well enough alone, after getting the pants beat off of us in Seattle. On a very morbid flight home, I got the dumb idea, although at the time it was a very bright and clever idea, to change the mood and make everyone laugh. So, I proceeded to remove the white colored head cover off my seat and poked holes for eyes and a mouth. Now I've made a mask that has taken on the appearance of the K.K.K. (Oh, wow this gets better). I stood up and headed for first class with Billy and the rest of the coaching staff, as if I had some sort of a pass. Oh, my God, when Billy turned around he was furious as he yelled at me, "Go and sit your ass down now." Then he jumped up and followed me to my seat. As I sat down he yelled, "Shove that mask up your ass when you win twenty games, then you can do some shit like this." Well I couldn't shove the mask up my ass, so I did what I thought was the next best thing and shoved it in my mouth. I achieved my goal; the team busted up with laughter.

After Billy was done, I got an epiphany for the first time, as I sat there seriously pondering about winning twenty games. I just gained insight on Billy, as he was great at being managerial, and he was quite the quintessential. He just psychologically disciplined my behavior and at the same time he motivated me. It felt like a divine intervention—totally spiritual.

It wasn't a rumor that Billy also had a wonderful sense of humor. Here's another aspect of his humor combined with discipline, so this is how this soliloquy begins. We weren't playing very well and the one thing we could tell, losing makes Billy mad as hell. We were overdue and because of another loss he put us on a curfew. This meant to be in your room an hour and a half after the game. What that really meant was it pertained to everyone but a few. Again, I'll reiterate how Billy could display his sense of humor with discipline. After digesting this act of genius, it will astonish you on top of a grin. I was one of those few, along with Henderson, Murphy, and Armas. Chicago has the infamous Rush Street, that's where the nightclubs, bars, and stars are and the elite. So, if partying is what you want to do, Rush Street is the place to be, with lots of women to see, it's hard to beat. Not quite New York but it definitely can compete. It's gotten late, as a matter of fact, it's now 3:00 a.m. and I decide to turn in. I get back to the hotel and immediately the doorman rushes and opens the door for me. As I'm approaching the elevator, the doorman again rushes up to me and asks for my autograph. So, I said sure, no problem; he appeared so emphatic. I took the ball and noticed he had only two signatures on it, Dwayne Murphy's and Steve McCatty's. I signed it and gave it back to him. Little did we know that "Mr. Dramatic" the doorman would turn out to be somewhat problematic.

The next day at the ballpark as soon as I get there I was told Billy wanted to see me. I immediately knew it had to do with that darn curfew, and that in itself was true. Now I'm trying to figure out how in the heck he knew. As soon as I walked into his office, I was invited to sit down. He reached into his desk drawer and tossed me a baseball. It was the same baseball the doorman had me sign, except it had the time we arrived at the hotel on it. Steve McCatty—3:05 a.m., Dwayne Murphy—3:07 a.m., and Mike Norris—3:35 a.m. I was left in total disbelief as he had the unmitigated gall to come up with a contrived and devised ploy. Even employed, the doorman deployed him, as we were decoyed. His method was quite congenial, in between assertive and aggressive, and the results were pretty impressive.

This next soliloquy is a true testament to his great propensity and managerial abilities, with his immense capabilities. We were in Seattle and the great base stealer, Maury Wills, at the time attempted to manage. He went to drastic measures and extremes to get an advantage. He started with excessively watering down first base. That evidence wasn't hard to trace, the Giants did that to him in efforts to stop him from stealing second base. Now he's trying to stop Rickey on the way to his record setting pace. The game starts and the first and second inning go by. Billy has a frown on his face. Before the next inning starts, suddenly he calls time, as he sprints to home plate as if he's in a foot race. Oh, my God, Maury Wills had cheated and I can't even call this gamesmanship. I had never seen anything like this ever taking place. Billy is emphatic at home plate as he is gathered with the umpires pointing towards the ground. Billy argued so much with the umpires afterwards I didn't think he was going to stick around. He finally leaves and returns to the dugout safe and sound. I asked what happened, what he told me was totally profound. This was some severe and extreme egregious and ardent foul play.

After fifteen minutes of intense arguing, what I had witnessed with my own two eyes was well worth the delay. Maury Wills had moved the back line of the batter's box up closer towards home, which made it possible for the catcher to get closer to the pitcher to receive the pitch sooner. This enhanced the opportunity to throw Rickey out, who was attempting to steal. This ordeal was very protracted, the amazing presence of mind on how Billy reacted and he was responsible for how the game was totally impacted. The game was played under protest; may I suggest that this is another example of the man's genius at its best.

The pitching staff was comprised of five starters, led by me you couldn't find another staff that worked harder or smarter. These are their names in the order of the rotation: Norris, Langford, Keough, McCatty, and Kingman. I was blessed with the extraordinary ability labeled as athletic prowess, with the combination of power and finesse, a predator, an anomaly like my best pitch, the screwball. Langford had precision control with a big league slider, also a great athlete and was one heck of a competitor. My friend, the former *Oakland Tribune*, *Sports Illustrated* writer and columnist, Ralph Wiley, coined the phrase describing Rick Langford and I as the "Two Headed Monsters." Then there was the uniqueness and the cerebral approach of Matt Keough and his resilience from losing twenty games just the previous year. He featured a bona fide big league curveball and undoubtedly the best dry spitter in the game. Next there was our hard thrower, Mr. McCatty, possessing an above-average fastball with the ability to challenge hitters with it. He added a third pitch to his arsenal—the dry spitter, eventually making him one of the best pitchers in the league. Last but not least, was Brian Kingman. Everyone on the staff agreed he had the best stuff on the team. After losing twenty games that year was like a bad dream. You must be mentally tough to go through something like that, so extreme, while maintaining your self-esteem. He and McCatty didn't quite gain Billy's trust and that was a must. So, when one of them got 2-0 on the batter, they had to throw fastballs, which everyone in the ballpark knew was coming. That way of thinking became automatic. They weren't too pleased initially, but being professionals they didn't let it become problematic. Art and Billy's pet peeve was "you can't catch a walk" and that wasn't just small talk. That was designed so that they would become more focused on getting ahead in the count. Again, Billy's genius keeps equating into a large amount.

This was Art and Billy at their best with this next scenario. I can remember, very vividly, a game in which I walked five batters. During this particular inning, I had walked two, and I had 2-0 on the hitter. Now I walk a little way down the mound trying to trace my tracks in the dirt to see if I'm landing consistently. Just then I hear time out called immediately and persistently, as Art waddles to the mound, with his beer belly (I imagine that made it a little hard to get around). Angrily, I asked what was I doing wrong, he hilariously replied, "God damn buddy, I don't know, but I'll tell you one thing, you're pissing Billy off." I laughed so hard I pretended to cough. Then came this calmness and serenity from his sincerity that was so comical, it relaxed me. Honestly, I'd be willing to attest, that Art's best asset and skill set was to get us to relax. This enabled us to perform to our max.

Art was from Converse, South Carolina, born in 1922. With a strong southern accent, and without knowing him, you could easily assume he was a redneck racist. But oh no, quite the contrary, he was quite decent. One day I told him I was going to come and visit him in the off season and he replied, "God damn buddy, when you get here if anybody asks who you are, just tell them you're my new gardener." As well as professionally, he truly was my partner. Art lived to the ripe old age of 84 and believe me there was no one that I enjoyed more.

There was another occasion when I realized Billy cared about one's health and wellness. It's early May and I'm scheduled to pitch in Cleveland. We were leaving the hotel passing through downtown on the team bus, and the temperature read 33 degrees. It's hard for me to concentrate on pitching when I can only picture myself about to freeze. At this point, I can't even be appeased!

The bus arrives at the ballpark that's called, "The Mistake by the Lake," (Lake Erie). There are some wet, misty snowflakes dropping. I'm in prayer mode that this won't in the immediate future be stopping. It's two hours until game time and I'm trying to figure how to get out of this without reason or rhyme, and I'm running out of time. Without further delay it's time to go out and play. Art and I take our walk from the clubhouse to under the stands that lead to the field on an extremely cold and overcast day. As we walk towards the bullpen the wind is about to blow me away. I looked at Art without hesitation and shook my head and said, "No way." Art agreed and said, "Okay, God damn buddy, now let's go tell Billy."

We get back to the clubhouse and knocked on Billy's door, he says come in. I entered with a concerned look; he immediately asked if I was okay. With a frown on my face I said, "Yes and no. Yes, meaning I'm okay and no meaning I can't pitch today." He asked why and I said, "I hope this doesn't sound too cocky and bold, but I can't pitch because it's too damn cold!" He looked me dead in my eyes and said, "Okay, we'll skip you here and push you back to Toronto, it's got a dome. Your next start will be back at home." Just as simple as that, actually that's when he won me over. I just pray that this trust and confidence will at least maintain itself, or even better, carryover.

Professionalism and individualism created an aura of perfection, which is a fast track to unhappiness and depression. For example, you've pitched eight and one third innings and Billy calls timeout and comes to the mound and asks, "How do you feel?" I say abruptly, "I'm fine, now get the hell out of here and let me close the deal!" Was I having another epiphany, or was I attempting and completing games at a borderline rate of insanity? Through Billy's guidance, we as a staff acquired amity, no animosity or jealousy. We just went out every five days and pitched competitively, and that turned out quite successfully.

My very next start I experienced wildness again, it's the second inning and the bases are loaded with one out and I'm again retracing my steps to see if I'm landing consistently in the same spot. I hear timeout as I look up and see Billy approaching the mound in an urgent-type trot. The last start he lifted me after five and two thirds innings and before I could say I'm okay, he walked to me and said, "You Black S.O.B. quit fu__king around and turn this next pitch over and get a double play ball." So, the next pitch I turned it over and we turned a double play, as for Billy, again, the unmitigated gall. Billy knew who and what he could say to the staff. Instead of getting angry when he left the mound, I would just laugh.

Incidents like that make you no longer have to worry about getting sent down to AAA, which is 40 miles down the highway to San Jose. I used to frequently visit there because Mr. Finley advantageously exercised my options;

his purpose was to pick up supposed washed-up players. With uncanny consistency, he would be getting good production from most of them. Mr. Finley seemingly had a plan or scheme, which at times could be a little extreme. Especially when used to outwit an opponent or achieve an end. He was relentless and I've never ever known him to bend, his main objective overall was to win. Then he would sell them one by one, he being Charlie Finley, the previous owner prior to the Haas family that bought the team in 1980. There was no one like him on the planet Earth. You could never get out of him what you were really worth. In 1968 Dionne Warwick had a hit song entitled, "Do You Know the Way to San Jose?" My connection to this song is a dubious one, as I once pitched where the attendance was so low in Oakland from 1977 to 1979 when the fans yelled you could hear the echo! I could hear a fan in the centerfield bleachers, as he had something to say, "Hey Norris, do you know the way to San Jose?"

Now I have the ball every five days; with the ideology of every start I'm winning and going all the way. Time flies when you're having fun, we've been winning from the very beginning and now it's the All-Star break and we're in second place. This time last year we were in last place and were a complete disgrace. We went from second class to no class. No chartered flights, embarrassingly flying commercially waiting in airports impatiently. Having to be reduced to the usage of showering with no more than two towels. It angered one player to the point instead of toilet paper, he threatened to use the towels to wipe his bowels. I know that's gross, after that every time I'd see him I felt like giving him the Mr. T. growl (Oooah sucker!).

Here is your not so typical oxymoron, as I saw a clubhouse pee-on turned into a musical and global icon. Ladies and gentlemen, I bring you M.C. Hammer. This was awfully good, the owner, Mr. Finley, named him Vice President of the team, at the ripe old age of seventeen. He still lived with his mother in the hood. These were all indications that a once proud and multi-championship organization, is now in the midst of total degradation.

In with the new and out with the old, thank God the team got sold. We as a team were newlyweds and the wicked witch was dead. The new ownership, the Haas family was class personified. The sales of blue jeans made them very wealthy and along with that came a lot of pride. They simply behaved with sincerity, calm grace, generosity of spirit, and complete natural humility. We are no longer afflicted by pointlessness, fruitlessness, or uselessness that describes futility. We were like one big happy family. They would even socially interact, as well as transact your contract.

It's the All-Star break and I'm 10-5 and didn't get chosen to play in the All-Star game. Instead of playing, I was summoned by the American League President, and some league officials for throwing at the hitter Ben Oglivie, allegedly hitting him intentionally. Therefore, I was to attend a meeting in the same hotel where the All-Star teams stayed in which the league paid for. We can hopefully take care of this fairly and expeditiously. This has the makings of a soap opera soliloquy.

On a warm summer night in Milwaukee, playing against the Brewers, at the time were owned by ex-Commissioner Bud Selig, I was sitting directly behind home plate in the stands as Billy would let us chart the hitters the night before we pitched from there. Mr. Selig's daughter was sitting directly behind as I was totally unaware. Steve McCatty, who possessed an above average fastball, was pitching and getting hit extremely hard. Witnessing this, I had to try and ignore the body of evidence

that was too substantial to disregard. The offensive prowess they've shown this season, is the reason they've been
named after their manager, Harvey Kuenn, and the alcoholic beverage known as a "Harvey Wallbanger." This was
a very clever accurate depiction and cliché.

After five innings, I was angry and dismayed at the
way we played, while getting up to leave what I said displayed a slight lack of class. I said out loud to myself,
"Tomorrow I'm going to have to bust some ass." Obviously,
not knowing Mr. Selig's daughter, Wendy, was close
enough to hear what I said and went back and told her
daddy. Apparently, he received that bit of information surprisingly and quite delightedly.

Now this has turned into a full-blown witch hunt and
I'm left solely to bear the brunt. A witch hunt is where a
person decides to target another person for reasons that
may or may not be obvious. Essentially, it is a targeted attack against one person for reasons that aren't necessarily
tangible. Trying to find someone to target and humiliate, I
was having a hard time trying to differentiate. I was in between something transparent as palpable and something
perceptible by touch being tangible, or is this simply meta-
phorical, not having real existence but representing some
truth about a situation? One thing for sure my anticipation
and expectations have created some heightened suspense, because tomorrow's meeting I'm not prepared either with an offense or defense. So instead of pitching in
my very first All-Star game in the infamous Chavez Ravine,
better known as Dodger Stadium, I am attending this meeting. Being a Giants fan growing up, pitching there would
have been like a dream.

The time has come as the meeting has started, and all
the gentlemen introduce themselves and they all appeared
to be respectful and lighthearted. The first question right

out of the gate was, did you hit that batter with the intent to harm him? My answer was "No," without any hesitation or emotion. I had the presence of mind to answer the questions with the least amount of information about my conversation. Then I was asked could I elaborate more? I replied, "Sure, according to our scouting reports, you must pitch to Mr. Oglivie inside hard, as he's very quick inside, and has the ability to pull the best of fastballs. What makes it difficult to pitch to him is he crowds the plate, basically taking over the inside part of it. Attempting to make sure you get it inside sometimes you hold on to it too long and I accidently hit him in the knee. If you are attempting to brush a hitter back, then you throw it from the waist up to the shoulder. Making it strategically and advantageously for him standing so close to the plate, there is no other recourse, other than to pitch him away and let him own you. Other than that, comically speaking, you have the choice of becoming mad or irate. I am not the villain; it is he who dares your manhood not to throw inside!" Unfortunately, accidently hitting Mr. Oglivie caused him to miss two games.

Well with that answer they appeared to be satisfied, "I did a good job," they all replied. My day had brightened, as I felt I even left them somewhat enlightened! Now that it's all said and done, it was finally time to take a break at the All-Star break. Major League Baseball has given me two rooms and two tickets to the All-Star game in which I brought my loving and well deserving mother. I felt blessed to go through this ordeal with no one other than my mother.

After the break, I vowed that I would definitely make next year's All-Star team. I also was determined to prove that the first half of the season wasn't a fake. Winning 20 games at the least is at stake.

In the month of July, I went 5-1 with a 2.43 ERA in 50.2 innings. Now that's getting off to a good start and as ace of the staff, I'm quite proud that I'm upholding my part. Just continue to pitch while making it look like classical art. Again, time flies when you're having a good time, we're now in Minnesota and I have a lady friend there that's extremely fine. I was scheduled to pitch the next day so we had room service as she was wined and dined. Then afterwards we're having sex, and I heard something pop in my knee. It hurt like hell and it started swelling up, and now I'm wishing I had declined. The first thing comes to mind, is what am I going to tell Billy. After pondering for a while, all I could come up with was the truth, heck I even had the lady and my knee as proof. So, I call his room and he answers and I said, "Billy, this is Norris, sorry to bother you. I was having sex and I heard something pop in my knee and it's swollen a little bit." Now there's silence on the phone momentarily, then he says, "Okay, I've done that before, come to the park early for the next couple of days and get treatment. You should be ready to pitch the last game here." It was simple as that; you tell the truth to Billy and you have nothing to fear.

So, it's time to pitch and thanks to our trainer, the now deceased Joe Romo, and with immense therapy, I was ready to go. I rewarded Billy's decision by pitching 11 innings, giving up only 6 hits, 1 walk, 6 strikeouts, and only allowed 1 unearned run for my 16th win. I just need 4 more wins for 20 with only 6 starts left, and I'm going to do my best to achieve my quest. I'm no longer going after 20 with wonderment and curiosity, but I'm attacking this with some fierce ferocity.

As the countdown begins we'll move right along to my 17th win. I won 3 games in a row for 15, 16, and 17, by the same scores 2-1. I beat the Mariners for my 16th going 9 innings, 7Ks, gave up 3 hits, 2BB, 1 run and 1ER. My 16th was against the Twins winning 2-1 going 11 innings, gave up 6 hits, 6Ks, 1BB, 1 run and 0ER. My 17th was against the Red Sox with present Hall of Famer, Dennis Eckersley, who was a starting pitcher before La Russa turned him into arguably the best reliever of all time. That's easily said without reason or rhyme. We were both from the Bay Area, he being from Fremont and me from San Francisco. We had a lot in common, we also played on the same semi-pro team in San Francisco very briefly. He was one year older than I and was said that he threw harder than me. So automatically, I turned this into a competitive rivalry, so that victory was especially gratifying. I pitched another gem and that's what it took to defeat him, again winning 2-1. I went 8.2 innings, 3Ks, 7 hits, 1BB, 1 run and 1ER. On to 18 as I beat the Yankees at home in front of a sellout crowd of 50,000 plus 9-1. I was working on a no-hitter going into the ninth as Oscar Gamble hit a blooper, a Texas leaguer just over the outstretched glove of our shortstop to break it up. I was quite angry but I kept my composure so that I could finish the game with closure.

The heat and the humidity turned out to be my toughest opponent as I started off the month of August in Baltimore back east. In the heat of the night it was heck of a fight, despite the heat and humidity, that night my stuff was like electricity. For the first time, I didn't resist coming out of the game, my body just didn't feel the same. I was exhausted mentally and physically. All that hard work and I wound up with a no decision, as we lost and that was something I didn't envision. I went 7.2 innings, I only gave up one hit and it was a solo home run, 5Ks, 2 runs, 1ER, with 4BB.

We leave the humidity and come home against the Rangers. I go 9.0, 4Ks, 5 hits, 1 run, and 1ER. While getting the win my 19th, I'm just one win away then it's on to Texas and the heat is on literally. It was down to 97 degrees at game time, which was 7:30 p.m. I had to become prepared mentally so that I would last physically. You must hydrate with lots of water, fruit, and the trainer prepares a bucket of ammonia water with ice and a towel in it. Without all of this, it takes a lot of will not to quit. You'll find out if you're in shape, or even more so, how extremely fit you are. Talk about endurance, I pitched 11 innings, 10 hits, 3BB, 1K, 2 runs, and 2UR. I obviously didn't have my best stuff, but now I've proven to myself that I'm pretty damn tough!

The game is over; it's done and I won. I'm just a beginner at being a 20 game winner. To top it all off, the legendary broadcaster Keith "Whoa Nellie" Jackson interviewed me for the post game show. Now that I'm acquiring status quo, my next objective is to become a consummate pro.

I've got just three starts left and I've won my last 6 out of 8 to go 4-2 for the month of August, in route to winning my 20th. Then one night, I dreamed that the following year I won my 30th. To win 20 games was a dream come true and totally is a lifetime accomplishment, as I'm left extremely humbled and I remain in total astonishment. The question is, how did I get here to this point, and who deserves the credit with a compliment? He's the same person that got 25 guys on board to play and be on the same accord. Yes, Billy Martin, our resident genius and manager. What he brought to the table for me was that he was a challenger and an examiner. He brought out the best of our ability into a state of proficiency. What was hidden from the public's eye was a very compassionate guy. Understanding and rectifying a situation regarding the team or personnel, without even asking why. That's why when you take the field for him, you play so hard until you damn near die.

It's the month of September I went 3-1, 2.52 ERA, 45 IP, 24Ks, 39 hits,17 runs, 18ER, 7HR, 14BB. I beat Kansas City 9-3, for my 21st. Then back home to Oakland where I did something that was against my standards. I lost a game while ahead, instead of going onward and forward I took a step backwards. We lost to those pest-like nemesis, the Milwaukee Brewers, 11-7, as they scored 6 runs in the 9th with 2 outs. I couldn't get that last out as I literally ran out of gas while they tore me a new ass. I did complete the game but when it was over I did feel embarrassment and shame. Although I did complete the game going 9.0 with 7 Ks, gave up 9 hits, 11 runs, and 2BB, it was a game to forget and totally disclaim.

It's the first day of October and my last start, as once again Billy showed his compassion and care as he gave me two extra days in between my last start. Right on cue as he always does his part, he has a big heart. That extra day's rest apparently made me stronger and revitalized as I victimized the White Sox 11-3 going 9.0, giving up 9 hits, with 7Ks, 3 runs, 3ER, and 2BB for my 22nd win. As for my season, it came appropriately and professionally to an end. My final statistics were as follows: 22-9, ERA 2.53, 284 IP, 180Ks, 215 hits, 80ER, 88 runs, 18HR, and 83BB.

Here are my road and home facts, regarding my affect and impact. I pitched 15 games at home. I had an ERA of 2.26, pitched 131.1 innings, allowed 104 hits, had 33ER, 36 runs, gave up 7 home runs, walked 29 batters, (1 intentionally) threw 4 wild pitches and balked 2 times.

On the road, I pitched 18 games, had ERA of 2.76, pitched 153 innings, allowed 111 hits, had 47ER, and 52 runs, 11 home runs, walked 54 batters, (1 intentionally) threw 5 wild pitches, hit batters 4 times, and balked 2 times.

What a year, as I reached some major milestones in my career! I attribute that to Billy for the opportunity and the care that was genuinely sincere, with the savvy of letting me be me, that was most important. I could exhibit my propensity through my intensity and immensity. I pitched well over 200 innings, which included completing games with a high rate of consistency. Not at any point did I feel overused or remotely abused.

During the off season, I faced a new challenge, I had to divert my generally pleasant thoughts of being amused to concentrating on the racism and politics that has left me somewhat confused. Politically and racially they are two separate entities, but when combined they can become a total mystery and even a lethal adversary. For example, there were three writers for the Cy Young Award voting and not one even voted for me, as they left me off the ballot entirely. Coincidentally and ironically, that's how many votes I lost by, three, and nobody knows how or why. It's just a bunch of speculators like me. If you think that was extreme with a record at 10-5, I was also left off the All-Star team. Actually, that happens to some unfortunate soul every year it seems. I'll just have to wait until next year to accomplish those dreams. Although I did win the first of two Gold Glove Awards, I guess the end justifies the means.

This political and racial crap is extremely critical and cynical, and those that are involved are hypocritical. The sad part is that all that ever comes out of this is absolutely nothing, because it's either viewed as immaterial or theoretical. Do you know that I wonder sometimes if those three writers were held accountable for suspiciously not voting for me? Not to be too candid, but personally I think they should have been reprimanded, or more specifically, suspended. I can't seem to get rid of that awful taste and smell out of my head that's extremely rancid and burns like acid.

The 1981 season was shaping up to be a great one, after winning my first five starts, but the season was interrupted by a strike. This led to a split season that shortened the 1981 MLB season, as a result teams only played between 102-110 games. This was perhaps the most devastating news that I could have possibly received. Had you told me this beforehand, it would have been something I wouldn't have believed. Coming into the season I was so focused and intense; I was going to win 30 games at any and all expense.

The month of April was great, 5-0 with a 2.14 ERA, 42IP, 23Ks, 25 hits,10ER,10 runs, 4HR, and 21BB, but in the month of May I suffered a different fate, going 2-3 with a 3.31 ERA, 42IP, 22Ks, 44 hits, 21ER, 25 runs, 6HR, and 14BB. This was a first time giving up more hits than innings, to that I can't relate. This didn't affect my confidence, but it slowed me down enough to contemplate.

It's now June and as it turns out this will be my last start before the strike. I can already tell that this is something I'm just not going to like. In the end, I pitched well enough to get the win going 1-0 with a 3.25 ERA, 7.0IP, 3Ks, 7 hits, 2ER, 2 runs, 0HR, and 5BB. I compiled a record of 9-3 at the end of the first half, as we're in first place as the division leaders at a record of 37-33 with a 617 winning percentage.

PRECARIOUS - not securely held in position, dangerously likely to fall or collapse. This is what it felt like to me after 30 days without baseball. It felt as if there wasn't going to be an end to this season at all. I no longer worked out, coming to the deduction that no strike ever lasted this long. That was totally and significantly wrong. In an unwise manner, not working out was done out of stupidity. That showed a lack of good sense and judgment, as I acted irresponsibly, which showed as well, as that was a lack of character and maturity.

The rise and demise of the Five Aces, as we were the envy of the league, and you would find most opposing pitchers who would love to trade places. From my perspective, this became provocative and somewhat suggestive. There are many numerous and various pieces of evidence that have led to this terrible incidence.

June 6th vs. the Red Sox as I shut them out for my 9th win. I didn't pitch again until August 11, which was a total of 63 days with no pay. We resumed the season by beating the Twins while pitching only 5 innings.

The very next start is where the trouble began. I pitched an 11 extra inning ballgame, before entering that game my ERA was a respectable 3.12. I had given up 7 hits, 1ER, 1 run, 2Ks, 1BB, and 0 homeruns. That's the game that took all my heart and soul, but in the long run it also took a toll. As for the very next start, I only lasted 5 innings, 7 hits, 6 runs, 6ER, 3 home runs, and 2BB. Five days later in Boston at Fenway Park I had another disastrous start, only lasting 2.2 innings before I was made to depart. Giving up 5 hits, 7ER, 8 runs, 1K, 4BB, and the only bright side of it was that I didn't let them hit one in that net or out of the park. This once vivid picture is now starting to turn dark.

In conclusion, the month of August ended like this: I went 1-2 with a 3.91 ERA, in 23.2IP, 6Ks, 22 hits, 17ER, 18 runs, 3HRs, and 8BB. This left me astonished and if this doesn't end soon, I'll be looking to soon be admonished.

Then came the month of September, another dreadful month that was despicable to remember. My first start is against the Indians and I lost but I battled and competed through 8.0 innings, giving up 6 hits, 2 runs, 0HR, 2Ks, and 2BB. I had good stuff and pitched well enough to win, but that to me didn't really matter because I lost again. My next start is against the Rangers since they're in the same division; they're no strangers. Career wise I've done well against them in the past, and I want this to continue to last. Well it did as I went 9.0 innings, gave up 7 hits, 1ER, 1 run, 1K, 1HR, and 2BB. Now I'm learning how to pitch to contact, producing a different approach on how the hitters react. They're swinging at my pitches early in the count out of fear of hitting with two strikes. As a matter of fact, it's making it so my control and hitting spots don't have to be so exact.

The very next start is against our rivals the Royals of Kansas City. I battled for 8.1 innings, gave up 8 hits, 4 runs, 4ER, 0HR, 1K, and 3BB. Afterwards, I felt that I had made too much contact with their bats. I continued participating and somewhat obliterating my stats. I'm inconsistent, I'm not staying the same throughout, and I must become more persistent. Psychologically, I'm getting a lift as we head to Texas. What I love most about Texas is having room service and ordering a good old Southern breakfast. It consisted of smothered chicken topped with country white gravy, hash browns, grits, with pancakes. This is the kind of fuel you need, instead of eating at McDonald's; a Big Mac, fries and a milkshake.

As I've stated before, I've had a considerable amount of success against the Rangers. Now I must take out some of my furies on them. Other intangibles must factor in such as comfortability, familiarity, responsibility and my recent history equals victory. My confidence is immense because the last time I was here, my 20th win took precedence. As expected from myself I pitched a gem, going 9.0, 5 hits, 5Ks, 1 run, 1ER, 0HR, and 3BB.

Now I can't wait for my next start, but it went as though I didn't prepare physically or mentally by reading the scouting chart. I'm pitching like the scariest roller coaster ride; I've lost two consecutive and very decisive games to the White Sox and this crap must subside. In the first game against the White Sox I went 6.1, gave up 10 hits, 8 runs, 8ER, 0HR, and 5Ks. This is erratic and I'm beginning to become quite emphatic, in turning this into being dogmatic. The next start ends in disbelief, as this is the second game in a row that I've needed relief. My record is now mediocre at 11-9 with a 3.96 ERA, this has made me more determined to make my soon-to-be victims pay. I need to avenge that loss to seek revenge.

Well it appears this next start will be my last in front of my home team crowd, as they'll be cheering nice and loud. So, let's see if I can thrill them and send them home happy and proud. Hallelujah! I finally won and it was done in quite a spectacular way, I must say. These were my stats on that day: 9.0IP, 3 hits, 4Ks, 0 runs, 0ER, 0HR, and only 1BB.

Now I can honestly and confidently say I'm finally in shape. Perhaps it's time to put my Superman cape back on? I had to get out of that funk and make an escape. Is the nightmare over of pitching terrible during this strike-shortened season? There is no doubt that not being in shape was the real reason. I had experienced a dreadful month of August, as these statistics don't lie. I went 3-4 with a 3.76 ERA, in 57.2, 24Ks, 47 hits, 22ER, 22 runs, 4HRs, and 15BB. Since that was my last start these became my final stats: 12-9 with a 3.76 ERA, 172IP, 78Ks, 72ER, 77 runs, 17HR, and 63BB. These are the statistics showing the production or lack of before and after the strike for the starting rotation:

PLAYER	BEFORE	AFTER	TOTALS
Norris	8-3	4-6	12-9
Langford	5-6	7-4	12-10
McCatty	7-4	7-3	14-7
Keough	6-3	4-3	10-6
Kingman	3-0	0-6	3-6

It appears that Kingman and I suffered the most from the strike stoppage, as the second half caused blockage. Since the season was split, Oakland won the first half and Kansas City won the second half, which created a one game playoff to determine who will play in the American League Championship.

Steve McCatty was actually having a better year than I. Billy reported to the local media that McCatty would open for the playoffs. Being the ace of the staff, that bit of news really ticked me off. Come to find out Billy purposely said that, knowing that I would possibly read it and become livid, but in this pressured arena one must be humble and lucid, while appearing luminously vivid. Again, there was the use of psychology in his methodology to motivate me. It worked, as there is no need to impede. As once again we were able to succeed. I felt immediate relief that we still had amity, as he named me the starter to open the playoffs against Kansas City. I heard later that he sarcastically replied when he found out that I could read. With my mental and physical, again feeling as one, I proceeded to go out and pitch, have fun, and the result was we won! Again, I pitched a masterful game in which I went 9.0 innings, scattered 4 hits, struck out only 2, walked 3 with 0 runs, 0ER, and 0HR.

It's extremely tough with all that pressure to succeed.

After that victory, shutting them out 3-0, we won and it felt like the weight of the pressure came off in tons.

Wow, the Oakland A's are playing for the American League Championship against the powerful New York Yankees. We must play sound baseball including a little gamesmanship. Again, I'm chosen to start the first game and I'm expecting the results to be the same. Well, things didn't exactly go as planned, as they scored three runs in the first. We offered strong resistance but were unable to withstand. The great and crafty Tommy John beat me 3-1; I basically lost the game in the first inning. It was uncanny that I actually lost a game from the very beginning. I went 7.1 innings pitched, gave up 6 hits, had 4Ks, only 2BB, 0 HR, 3ER, and 3 runs, with an ERA of 1.65. Although we didn't win, I pitched well enough to win, and oh my God what a disappointing way for my season to end!

We were eventually swept in all three games as McCatty was treated quite rude, crude and shrewd. Now we're down 0-2 in the playoffs and it looks like we're screwed. The Yankees had a well-balanced attack that we couldn't withstand, because basically we were simply just outmanned. McCatty lasted 3.1 innings, gave up 6 hits, 5 runs, 5ER, 2BB, and 2Ks as the Yankees went on to win 10-3. Game three was a well-pitched game by Matt Keough, but he couldn't get any offensive support due to injuries sustained to Henderson and Murphy quite early, as they had to leave the game.

After those turn of events, we as a team, lost focus, which was highly unlikely of us. We became tame and that's how we lost that game. In conclusion, we had a fantastic season and we have no reason to be ashamed. Unfortunately, and unknowingly, after this year, things won't ever be the same. Our invaluable right arms began to break down and it was as if we couldn't refrain. We had become addicted and insane in the brain, pitching past fatigue and severe physical pain.

Let's recap our demise statistically as our production decreased exponentially. In 1980, Rick Langford finished 28 of 34 and the last 28 in a row. I completed 24 of 33, Matt Keough completed 20 of 32, Steve McCatty 11 of 31, Brian Kingman 10 of 30. The next season, which is the strike season, was shortened to 109 games, the staff had 60 complete games, nearly doubling the 33 complete games compiled by the next closest team. Langford finished 18 of 24 games, McCatty 16 of 22, and I lagging well behind the pace of the previous season with 12 of 23. At the time, over the past 18 years, only one has matched my 1981 complete game total—that was Randy Johnson in 1999 with a 162 game season. 1980-1981 we had 154 complete games in 271 starts.

Pitch counts were kept but never used to determine when a starter is done. If you went 9 you usually won. Langford was the most economical of the staff. He would average 110 pitches in 9 innings, opposed to McCatty who usually threw between 130 to 140 pitches in complete games.

Sometimes we needed a lot more pitches than that. Langford, McCatty, Keough, and I each threw a 14 inning complete game in 1980 when we set a major league record with 94 complete games. I needed 152 pitches to get through my extra inning marathon. McCatty threw 207 and like myself, when Billy came to check on him, McCatty sent him marching back to the dugout. That scene was hilarious, because it either looked like we wouldn't let him in or we put him out. What made it so comical was that, McCatty and I were the only ones that were crazy enough to make Billy take that round-about route. Deep down inside Billy appreciated the slight tout.

The final nail in the coffin was the following spring training. Billy had a congenial idea as he invited the top prospects as far down as AA to learn the Billyball way. But, the whole team including the pitchers, didn't get enough innings and the opportunity to play. I left spring training with a minuscule 14 innings. The *New York Times* wrote—the Oakland A's would like the Mike Norris they had come to know, the pitcher with the fine control who won 22 games back in 1980, to step forward at their spring training camp in Scottsdale, Arizona. This year I have given up 10 walks, hit one batsman, thrown 5 wild pitches, and made a wild pickoff throw to first base all in 6.1 innings in 3 substitution games.

In the next game against Cleveland, 22 out of the 29 pitches were balls. I only walked 63 in 173 innings last year and 83 in 284 innings the year before. Our manager, Billy Martin, and pitching coach, Art Fowler, are worried. "He's in great shape," said Fowler. "But when you watch him you wonder what he's doing out there," Martin added, "He has absolutely no rhythm at all." Well there you have it, as this continued throughout the season and only myself can figure out the reason. I finished with a 7-11 record with an ERA of 4.67, in 166 innings, and 84 walks. That was as much as I had a year ago with 83 strikeouts. Now personally, mentally, and physically, I'm at an all-time low and acting somewhat pretentiously. Subconsciously, I was trying to mask my pain with the usage of cocaine.

Moving right along, the off season felt very prolonged, as I continued to do what was apparently wrong. Now it's a new season, 1983, and our once invincible staff has physically broken down one by one. Is it possible all of us are done? I suffered from a trapped nerve and severe tendonitis and pitched a total of 83 innings. Keough had 100, Langford 20, and Kingman 5 innings. McCatty wasn't healthy, but he led the way with 167 innings and a decent ERA.

I had a record of 4-5 with an ERA of 3.76 going into, unknowingly, what was my last start in the big leagues until my short return in 1990. Yes, it took 6 years but I made it to hell and back, thank God almighty.

The 1983 season is one I'll never forget as I had a total of just 19 innings in my previous 6 starts, averaging 3.2 innings per start. On my 16th start against the Twins, I can vividly remember how my arm began to hurt so darn bad in the third inning. Somehow, I got out of that inning as the nerves in my shoulder felt as if though they wanted to jump out of my right arm.

The inning is over and I'm back in the dugout and as soon as I sat down my arm began to shake violently and uncontrollably—this gave me great alarm! Sitting next to me was reliever Dave Beard, as he sat and witnessed me having to put my arm between my legs to stop it from shaking. Heck, no disrespect, but even Stevie Wonder could see that I wasn't faking. Now Dave Beard is pleading for me to tell Billy, but of course, I didn't. I was just being stubborn or just being plain dumb and silly. As I went out to start the third inning, I had stiffened considerably as if my body deliberately said no I've had enough. Instead my ego kicked in, so I proceeded to be tough, but that turned out unpleasantly rough.

It's time to swallow my pride, because this pain isn't going away; it's here to reside. Warming up to start the inning was excruciating as it felt like I was experiencing a dead-like feeling of rigor mortis. My movements became as slow as a tortoise. The next inning began and my first pitch was very high and outside; I knew right then I would need to choose between my career or bravery. The very next pitch I experienced displacement, as my back and shoulder felt as if they were no longer adjacent. Oh my God, this is the kind of pain you just can't hide! Please believe me, I sure as heck tried. As I left the mound to a nice ovation I realized this was a different type of adulation. I almost cried. Sitting in the clubhouse pondering about my career and bleak future, quite frankly, left me in tears! Little did I know, that was going to be my last game in the big leagues for the next six years.

It was true, A's pitchers led the league in complete games and innings pitched for two years. We were breaking ball pitchers who normally put balls into play before going deep in the count. Our low pitch count per game (often in the 90-100 range) was better than average and a better barometer of our actual workload.

Nobody in the media was counting pitches 25 years ago, and the A's didn't have that information. With a fair degree of accuracy, they could estimate the number of pitches thrown by a starting pitcher, thanks to a tool devised by a sabermetrician who goes by "Tangstiger."

We were routinely throwing between 90 and 100 pitches, which is preposterous. Here are the estimated pitches from those two seasons broken down in groups of ten:

PLAYER	GAMES STARTED	90-99	100-109	110-119	120-139	140-149	150+
Norris	56	4	4	12	11	10	4
Langford	57	3	6	11	11	10	3
McCatty	53	2	5	12	9	3	4
Keough	51	4	4	9	6	3	4
Kingman	45	3	8	9	8	3	0

In another of Billy's books, he explained all the injuries to his Oakland pitching staff this way: "For two months I wasn't there and my pitching coach, Art Fowler, wasn't there either to see if my pitchers did their work, warmed up properly, did their running, wore a jacket when they were sweating, threw with the proper motions—all the things that managers have to watch to "baby" their pitchers." I'm convinced the sore arms that came later were the results of improper training during the strike, not overuse. So, there you got it, straight from the horse's mouth, confirming the probabilities on how things went south!

The numbers in the pitches column don't match exactly to the games started, because of course, occasionally we were knocked out before 90 pitches, but there were zero complete games of fewer than 90 estimated pitches, my lowest was 93. In fact, the five of us combined for only two complete games of fewer than 100 estimated pitches while Langford had the other low-pitched game of less than 100.

There's still another way to look at this. In our complete games, and of course there were a lot of them, how many pitches did we average?

PLAYER	CG	PITCHES/CG
Norris	36	131
Langford	46	129
McCatty	27	131
Keough	30	131
Kingman	13	126

"We didn't routinely throw in the 90-100 range," as Falkner claims. We routinely threw in the 120-140 range. We were certainly pitchers that could survive, or even thrive, under the yoke of each other's workloads. Most cannot survive, simply because what was expected mentally from of us was a lot.

Again, the genius was correct as well as direct, as none of the other starters have blamed Billy for allegedly being overused. Therefore, I felt I had to address this, because so many people are still confused. Every one of us had the mentality that if we had the chance to do it again, would we do it the same way, yes, and it wasn't in the slightest about pay. It was about a man who was the mainstay, who possessed an immense cachet. He was a manager with great knowledge, who taught us a unique style of play which enabled me to put my talents to work and receive exposure in my own stylish way. I was provided the platform and opportunity on the field for me to display. And for that, Billy, thanks and I love you, that's something I never got to say. I never perceived him as an impediment because the good Lord put him in my life for the betterment!

With all that being said I'm going to end this exactly the way we did after a home game victory. The music group Kool and the Gang's song played and all the fans stayed. They sang and clapped their hands to the party in the stands while the lyrics rang out... "There's a party going on right here, a celebration to last throughout the years. So bring your good times and your laughter too, we're gonna celebrate and party with you. It's time to come together, what's your pleasure? Everyone around the world come on! Let's celebrate, celebrate good times come on!" I was writing while singing the lyrics, tears of joy came from my eyes, it made me pause and realize just how great those times were, oh how I wish they could reoccur!

8. WHAT'S UP, MY NIGGA?

The Black race's plight
Continually has been a constant fight

Having to survive being demoralized and
Absolutely, undeniably horrified

The Latin word for Black is Negra
By the time Africans made it to America
It got changed to Nigra

As the hate grew bigger
Then the word became Nigger

Are Blacks still called the word Nigger?
After all these years, 244 to be exact 398 since 1619
They say the truth hurts, and that's a fact

While most races won't say the word to your face
By law and ignorance that sure would be out of place

So who really uses the word the most then?
It's the Black man and woman,
As well as their children and kin

My mother never used that word
So in my house it was not heard!

No other races openly degrade themselves
No one other than just ourselves

The Chinese don't call themselves Chinaman

The Japanese don't call themselves Japs

The Germans don't call themselves Krauts

The Jews don't call themselves Heimi

The Italians don't call themselves Wops or Dagos

The Filipinos don't call themselves Flips

The Mexicans don't call themselves Wetbacks

The Puerto Ricans don't call themselves Spics

The American Indians don't call themselves Redskins

Why not? Because it's insulting and humiliating,
Degrading, frustrating, embarrassing, harassing,
disturbing, and even agitating

None of these words leave you feeling positive
Only quite the opposite, totally negative

Even Middle Easterners are called Sand Niggas

Can you picture a Middle Easterner
Greeting another with, "What's Up, My Sand Nigga?"

Neither can I!

Part 2

Brought over on ships shackled in chains,
Enduring total discomfort and immense pain.

Not counting the ones that died from various
Sickness and then thrown overboard,

To the horror of a loved one who's only comfort
Was to pray to the Lord.

As the saying goes "only the strong survive"
Which meant whomever made it to their destination alive

America the land of the free and the home of the brave,
To the Blacks they learned it meant being lynched,
From a tree and the new home for a slave and a possible
grave.

A slave was sold to a duplicitous man who became his
master,
A trade they called slavery, what a disaster!

Then Master proceeded to divide the Blacks and conquer

First by making them all address him as Master or yes Sir,
Then he took the light-skinned Blacks and the dark-
skinned Blacks and divided them

The light-skinned Blacks were house Niggers
and the dark-skinned Blacks were field Niggers

Not because working in the field was fun,
Because the light-skinned Blacks didn't work
As well in the sun.

Which created jealousy and immense envy,
Master having sex with your wife enhancing
Your misery and humility.

This was one of the greatest examples of
Divide and conquer in the history of slavery.

We persevered through our faith,
Determination, and bravery.

Although in the end slavery didn't win, it never does
Again, the Heavenly Father freed his children,
That's all it was.

It doesn't matter what kind of demon or who you are,
Whether your name is Hitler, Master, or King Pharaoh.
The Father through Moses said,
"Let my people go."

Then the blessing came,
When President Abraham Lincoln signed his name.

To free the slaves with a document called
the Emancipation Proclamation.

History makes the decision sound morally,
The truth of the matter it was done politically.

Slavery lasted long enough and that's a fact,
244 miserable, deplorable years to be exact.

Oh, but the newly freed Black had another rude awaken-
ing,
Again, Blacks had to experience a different
Kind of forsaking.

Not being able to read or write,
They couldn't find a job nowhere in sight.

So back to the plantation to be Niggas again

Swallowing your pride going back to Master
Asking for your job back

And when do you begin
30 years go by and now it is the 20th century

As they migrated North,
A new and better life came forth.

Blacks became musicians and entertainers,
They had bank accounts instead of burying
Their money in a Folgers coffee can container.

They owned automobiles and even homes,
Some could even afford telephones.

Realizing the significance of education
And even thinking about college

But that took money as well as knowledge
Now feeling somewhat economically empowered
It seemed nothing could stop Blacks from going forward

This was the 20's, 30's, and 40's in Harlem and Chicago

In New York's Harlem, which started across 110th Street,
Nightclubs jamming to blues or jazz to the hip, new beat.

Oh no! Master has returned again,
But this time he has a new friend.

Instead of Master doing the killings,

He found something else always willing.

Drugs the Nigga killer
Heroin is his name,
Death and destruction
Is his game.

It can turn you into a robber or murderer,
Sounds familiar, do I need to go any further?

Oh no! Back to being Niggas again,
Except now it is Black on Black crimes.
Now the parents are making the children,
Victims of hard times.

Through their inability
By not taking responsibility

Not getting their upbringing appropriately,
There goes the neighborhood.
Maybe they should save it, if they could.

Meanwhile back down South things,
Are still looking dim.
Chances to seek or gain decent employment,
Is relatively and virtually slim.

Still the best jobs for Blacks were subservient,
Some working for a few years and some made it permanent.

Then the sixties came, what a negative impact that had on
me.

As America watched Negroes hosed, beat on with billy
clubs,
Attacked by dogs and arrested on national TV.

Their houses and churches were burned to the ground,
Leaving you with a burning cross in what's left of your front
yard.
The scars from that terrible memory can only produce a
frown!

Can't go to the law, that wouldn't be the way,
Because they are the KKK.

So being a Black person you had to deal
With discrimination and segregation

Discrimination is tough,
And segregation is really rough.

White only bathrooms,
The only way a Negro could go in to it
Is if they had a mop or a broom.

White drinking fountains,
As if the water came out of the mountains.
Not really, they just didn't want your Black lips to touch the
fountain.

Then one day a woman named Rosa Parks had enough,
She took a stand for all of us.
No way, no how was she sitting in the back of that bus.

Then there was an Alabama Governor named George
Wallace,

BLACKBALLED TWICE

Standing front and center.
With Alabama State Troopers at the front door
Denying several Black students to enter.

He showed America his ignorance and hate,
As he later experienced his own terrible fate.

That being he was shot and became paralyzed,
There went his career as he became immobilized.

So enough about that demon,
The good Lord avenged him and got even.

Before he left this Earth, he had a change of mind,
I heard he looked for Jesus and he wasn't hard to find.

Then the good Lord blessed us with a whole new thing,
It came in the form of a man named Martin Luther King.

This man stood and died for his beliefs,
In a non-violent approach for justice and equality for all
With him as our leader there was a sense of relief.

Not at any time did this man come up small,
Everything he did with pride and dignity as he stood tall.
His mission on Earth was to most definitely answer God's
call.

Although along his journey he faced extreme danger and
humility,
He never lost sight of the goal and that was to be free.

Repeatedly arrested and thrown in various southern jails,
Sometimes he stayed for long periods of time without bail.

Can you imagine that must have been a living hell?

This man led 300,000 people to march on our nation's capital
To protest segregation and discrimination

He left us with possibly the most significant speech,
In the history of America's past.
As he spoke those climactic words "Free at last, free at last,
Thank God almighty, we're free at last!"

Then he returned to the very next year in 1964
As President Lyndon B. Johnson passed the
Civil Rights Bill, ending segregation and discrimination

Shortly after all of this, they ended Martin Luther King's bliss,
For he was assassinated
It happened too soon as for the second time we got emancipated.

We were all in remiss,
Now he ceased to exist.

That duplicitous James Earl Ray killed our leader,
Right before his death he said he had seen the Promised Land
And I'm a believer!

We didn't get to thank Dr. King while he was here,
For the day you left us I shed a tear.
I always love and admire you for enduring
The pain and sorrow that you went through

For you had many deterrents, but one of them wasn't fear,
I will always disseminate your message for others to abide
and adhere.

That's why when you spoke, I always wanted to hear,
What you had to say with my own two ears.

For me, you were my teacher, mentor, and preacher,
While these were some of the gifts you were blessed with
And could proudly feature.

You were more than a mere friend,
You fought for all of us through thick and thin.
I'm praying one day my heart will properly mend,
Because the name King and the word Nigga just don't
blend.

It's something I can't comprehend,
Let's make it end.

In Summary:
Parents teach your children that the word Nigga is a curse
word basically. It should be treated as if it were a sin.

Webster's dictionary definition of sin: an immoral act considered to be a transgression against divine law.

Synonyms are: immoral act, wrongdoing, act of evil, wick-
edness, transgression, crime, offensive, misdeed, or mis-
demeanor.
Slavery was comprised of murder, rape, lust and hate,
Think of all the Blacks that have succumbed to this fate.

All the whippings and beatings,

And the limited and unhealthy servings for feeding.

Then the Master had the nerve to cut off limbs and other body parts,
According to your so-called sins.
Let's see—where do we start or begin?

If you were caught stealing, they cut off your hand,
If you tried to run away to escape, they take off your foot.

If you were caught with the Master's wife,
That could very well be the end of your life.

If you were to survive all this,
There is no bliss.

Our youth don't understand the toils and strife,
This is why they are having such difficulties in life.

History is so important
If you don't know where you came from
Then how are you going to know where you're going?

They must start by respecting themselves,
By doing better than they are doing.

For those of you that want knowledge, get some,
Instead of sitting around getting high, letting your brain go numb.

We need to have more scientists, engineers,
Doctors, lawyers, administrators, and politicians
Not thieves, crack heads, alcoholics, and murderers.
It just leads to more convictions

Youth must get a good education,
So you can prosper and not get caught up
In some of life's repulsive devastation.

9. EXTENSION OF THE BLACK LEGACY-POEM

Through my extensive research and due diligence, I've come to a significant discovery and conclusion. The lack of Blacks in Major League Baseball is not an illusion. The research that's required for this is like dealing with immunity. This has all the makings of a dramatic mystery. To get a better understanding and a sense of this, to obtain the truth, I must persist. There's the quest as I'm in pursuit of, the factual truth, and that I can't resist. I realize that this subject can be viewed as highly controversial and exclamatory.

For this information, I had to backtrack, and revisit our legacy and history. God bless Mr. Branch Rickey, although his good intentions weren't totally moral. It had more to do with issues racially and economically. Abraham Lincoln had the same distinction, but his was done more politically. To me, the integration of baseball is tarnished and misleading historically. Speaking of historically, I mean this literally, the signing of Black ballplayers is basically back to how it used to be initially.

In the case of Jackie Robinson, as he was referred to as a *Nigger*. He was the first Black "to be the right kind of Nigger." Who could take the pressure of being the first Black and perform? All of this was way out of the norm despite being totally affected. He had to do all of this in order to conform. It wouldn't have worked if he was indecisive or had a personality like a bad storm. He was quite the opposite, even though just being

Black, he was at a deficit. Although Jackie had one heck of a resume, and to that I say touché. He received a college education at UCLA. He then enlisted in the Army of the U.S.A. He was the epitome and the prototype. "But, if he's Black, the Blackman cannot become psychologically White." That's the type of individual a racist will have fear of and fright of. Now do you see why the slaves weren't allowed to read or write? The fact of the matter was Jackie wasn't the best Black player to choose from, but he was the most qualified.

Josh Gibson and Satchel Page were bigger stars and heavily scouted, but for various reasons they were nullified. When it came to character, Jackie was the most dignified. It basically boiled down to personality and characteristics. Jackie excelled in bravery, intelligence, and most of all he was well disciplined. Most importantly, he open-mindedly listened to what they had to say and from his military background he also knew how to obey. That's what it was going to take for this experiment to work, and for him to succeed to stay and play. Ironically, to my surprise, these are the same characteristics the Black player coincidently must have these days. So, there's more scrutiny and less opportunity, let's see where we can find the origin. No pun intended, but I see this has taken the form of transparency. I can see through this soliloquy; it now needs some buoyancy.

Owners—you're sinking and having a difficult time competing and staying afloat. You can no longer sit back, count your money and gloat. You have a pattern of greed, your desires are greater than your family's needs, unlike your employees worries of how many mouths they must feed. To experiencing getting cut twenty percent and cold heartedly refuse our plead. In the early seventies, there was an influx in the signing of Black players out of burned down Watts and newly rebuilt Compton. Escaping from being in gangs such as the *Bloods and Crips*, just so you can play ball. Peer pressure is another trip trying to fit in and be hip.

The same thing transpired in the ghettos of the East Bay, ultimately, having to sign for less money. In the end, they were released with no money and no college education, that's not very redeeming nor funny! Returning to poverty, not power, because of the lack of opportunity in their community. As owners, you're quite aware of the advantage you have, exploiting young naïve Blacks and other minorities. I understand it's a business and I get the concept, but it doesn't make it any easier to accept. Just another one, who aspired of playing in the big leagues one day. Little did he know the odds were against him even though he could play. Your worth is determined by your pay, which controls how long you stay. You would have to be twice as good when you're Black, than a White player, then you'll get to the big leagues without much delay. As a contestant, you've become an investment, which makes you a monetary asset that will provide income in the future.

Owners—economically you just switch hats and become the executioner. This is the same method the previous owners used when they violated the Negro Leagues and the Caribbean. I find this quite illuminating that this involves cultures that were ravished by slavery, all dark-skinned who were Africans. Let it be told we're still being bought and sold, now we're just high-priced slaves. That's why there are so few of us, what happened to the owner's lust?

My findings are somewhat understandable from an economic perspective, why there is a lack of Black African-Americans. I estimate from 1978-1986 there was, what I call, the cocaine era. The FBI was called in to investigate in 1981 but, it felt more like Watergate. Some high-profiled Black stars went to prison and many others were black-balled systematically. This is called internalized racism, it's a form of racism of systematic oppression, affecting people and communities. Ever since then, this machination has worked and this is the residual. You're not discriminating against all Blacks, just uneducated ones. It's a business decision, which is causing the division and blocking our vision. I get it, you're no longer going to waste money on a bad investment. That is as clear and definite as a will and testament. What would be fair and equitable to both parties is to pay for the player's college education. That's if you sign him out of high school, and if he goes under the fifth round in the nation. Although your preference would be for them to play in college, for on and off the field they'll have the necessary tools and knowledge. They are much more mature, physically and mentally. They have a little better understanding about finance and romance. These are the things they need to embrace and enhance. Ignorance doesn't produce knowledge or prepare you for college. Even the ineffective MLB's RBI program [with all due re-spect] includes a reading component. You've come to real-ize ignorance is your opponent. I've noticed this from watching Black players on TV these days. Their articulation comes across instinctively well from interviews to commer-cials.

There is no doubt an educated person can achieve and advance much more rapidly. While applying these principles to baseball, perhaps from excelling so well, the Hall of Fame will give him that call. Going in wearing your team's jersey and the rest is protocol. MLB and owners, I know you are basically the same entity. You have an in-credible relationship, all of you but one have the same eth-nicity. Can't you see this is all about what's not being done for Blacks racially? This is America, the land of second chance and opportunity. This isn't just about baseball; it's about prospering and compassion while contributing to society. It brings back the hope to the community we have right here, in the East Bay. Oakland specifically has 400-600 youth from the Cal Ripken, RBI, and Babe Ruth Leagues ages 6-14. There are another 500-600 to a potential goal of 1,000 Black kids in neighboring counties that could play.

I currently have a travel ball league in progress to facilitate our vision, but with very little funding we're experiencing a paralyzing delay. We need someone to step up to the plate for that, I hope and pray. I work with three organizations besides my own, one is *Youth Sports Nation*. It is an incredible group of legends; Fred Biletnikoff, Raymond Chester, Bill Russell, Joe Morgan, Vida Blue, Bip Roberts, and singing sensation Lenny Williams. This organization was started by Terry Butler, music mogul and entrepreneur. He's joined forces with the Oakland Unified School District and we go to the schools and speak about the advantages of playing sports as well as education.

Then there's the highly acclaimed mentoring and tutoring program called the *Peacemakers*. We're currently working on a contract in Richmond, California, that's twenty minutes outside of Oakland. It will be a part of my travel ball league. I just recently was invited to speak at a banquet for the State Championship football team. After it was over, while talking to them, many of players said this is like a dream. These are young Black youth that have a school enrollment of 73% and 12.5% of the population is Black. The very next city over from them is Richmond with 31.4% of the population is Black with a 26.6% school enrollment. Do you see the disparity and very little diversity? There is the possibility they might go to a junior college and others will attend a university. These are the requirements and the necessary actions to resurrect a community.

Next are the infamous *Black Aces*; a group of only sixteen African-Americans in the history of Major League Baseball to win twenty games in a season. We have successfully partner shipped with NY Liberty Mutual in Binghamton, NY; Vida Blue, J.R. Richard, Al Downing, myself, and Mudcat Grant, the founder/co-author of the book *The Black Aces*. We annually support a very well put on event—our upcoming tenth annual Jim Mudcat Grant Golf Tournament. The proceeds go to various youth organizations and charities in Broome County.

I understand the necessity of good health, which is a large disparity compared to other communities. There is a silent killer amongst us living quietly with invisibility. It's called *Sarcoidosis*. It's hard to detect and has a deadly effect. When it came to race, personally, this slapped me in the face. African-Americans have a higher incidence of Sarcoidosis and women between the ages of twenty to fifty.

The disease of Sarcoidosis is the growth of tiny collections of inflammatory cells in different parts of your body. They are most commonly the lungs, lymph nodes, eyes and skin. Once again, there is a mysterious health threat that we must fight and win. There is a non-profit organization called *The Ann Weaver Foundation*. My era was an evolution so to speak, which left a lot of time for me to critique. We had to make a resolution to come together as one and be the solution.

The ball only bounces if it hits the ground, so let's go upwards not down. MLB and owners—you basically are the same entity. Your main interest is brand identity. There's the act of decency that reflects positively towards humanity. It appears you would rather prosper with another country instead of our own. Will the Cubans be your next clones? This great country changed for the better due to two great Black men; Jackie Robinson and Martin Luther King Jr. Our youth somewhat try to emulate us so we must lead by example and do the right things. We need more of our Black youth in this generation to prosper through education. So, when the time comes for contracts and negotiations, you'll be on the same level of communication. I must reiterate this is America the land of second chances and opportunities. It's a place where a person can improve upon one's life. Remove some, if not all the strife, your deficiencies, inadequacies, and insecurities. To be able to come back and give one's time financially and physically, to make it more prosperous in your community. The uselessness, pointlessness, and ineffectiveness is futility.

Mike Norris
A'S • PITCHER

10. BRINGING OUR YOUTH, THE TRUTH

I have so much information to share and it's very sensitive and extensive. So, I've put it in a poem to make this more enjoyable and comprehensive. I'm not trying to embarrass or put our youth on blast, but in education, incarceration, addiction, and death, we're first in being the worst. These things that we need to excel in; we are coming in dead last. Is this the residual from slavery's past? There is a very old saying, "The truth hurts." To find out those truths, just how much energy are you willing to exert? Our knowledge of our African roots and heritage is embarrassing and checkered at best, basically and completely devoid of it and deceitfully engaged in distorting, changing, and defaming. But there is an immense amount of lies and in this book, I am going to expose the ten best lies of African-American history, while bringing our youth the truth.

1. Whites were the first people on Earth.
2. Blacks in slavery were only cotton pickers and maids.
3. Lincoln freed the slaves.
4. Blacks ate each other in Africa.
5. Blacks were cursed black by God.
6. The United States government has helped Blacks succeed.
7. Jews built the pyramids.
8. Blacks sold other Blacks into slavery.
9. There was no slavery in the North.
10. Columbus discovered America.

(Please research "The Final Call" www.finalcall.com to obtain more insight on the ten best lies of African-American history.)

The goal is to get our pride and self-esteem back as a race that's worth regaining, because mentally, physically, and most of all spiritually, we've got a lot remaining.
So youth, I brought you the truth. Now, what are you going to do with it? One thing for sure, you better not quit. Take advantage of these blessings and do something with it. Much love, stay blessed, and don't accept anything less than the best.

Today, we experience daily witnessing of the death or deaths of African-American males every day between the ages of 17 to 25. It's a shame, God bless their souls, they should still be alive. Wake up Black youth and get out of these streets, start by going to church one Sunday and look for some front row seats.

The next step is to find out what is cool and that's getting good grades in school. That's what keeps you off the streets being a fool. Life has more to offer than just trying to survive and stay alive.

Oh, let me be frank with you, or would you rather me not? Or, would you rather continue to walk around blind as though you forgot? Young African-Americans recognize your powers. You've turned young America into hip-hop. One day African-Americans, you can be proud to say this nation is yours and ours. In the meantime, there's no longer room for incarceration, they've got you in separation and out of circulation. African-Americans are leaders in that statistic of the nation. Education is the same because one out of four drop out, that's basically ignorant. What that is all about is self-elimination. You can't blame that on anyone else but yourself. Without education, you'll have poor articulation, which will produce a lack of communication. You won't be employed without any experience or have an occupation. You have no excuse that's good enough to not get your education. If you think you do, it's only a copout. This is why you're subject to being faced with being a dropout. Life is too short and no one is too long for it. So, whatever it is you're doing I hope and pray you quit.

I hate to sound repetitious and even emphatic, I'm just tired of seeing too much usage of drugs and alcohol, which makes you erratic. This isn't helping the situation; you're heading down a hopeless road to becoming an alcoholic and addict. I can almost guarantee to you that it's pretty much automatic. Now your whole life has become problematic.

So, with trying to establish a one-on-one relationship with the Heavenly Father you can pray daily and exercise your faith. While accomplishing this, it's vital to your future prosperity and healthiness. While in your infancy, growing confidently and stronger spiritually, you leave home in the morning headed to school but on the way, you stop and get high with another fool. Now you've missed school and your punishment is detention because this has now become a habit. Detention doesn't even get your attention. School is left with no choice but to give him or her a well-deserved suspension. You must exercise the continued possession, use, or control of something which is retention. Get rid of that demeaning stereotype of being loud, ignorant and lazy. Every time I hear that, inside, it drives me crazy! The only way to change these thoughts is to remove the non-productive behavior as it fades away until it becomes cloudy and hazy.

The way you do that is by getting to first base. That's where you get education. Then on second base, you'll find nutrition. Then when you get to third base, you'll receive mentoring. When you get to home that's safe and after you touch all the bases, that's wellness. This is the lifestyle that you must embrace. You must lead by example on how to contribute to African-American's future without haste that makes waste and how to become a much stronger race. Finally, turn these intimidating frowns into welcoming smiles on your face. You want to be accepted into society instead of actually being and feeling out of place. One of my favorite quotes, "It takes a village to raise a child." It appears to me that quotation, like clothes, went out of style. A great deal of our youth is without guidance and is running around beguiled.

African-Americans, we must focus on getting on the right track, and bring what is meant to be a strong and prosperous community back. Along the way you have accumulated some great qualities; dedication, sportsmanship, respect, and a better understanding of being proud to be Black.

After touching all the bases and getting home, look back at all your accomplishments and acknowledge how much you've grown. If you weren't aware of this, the Heavenly Father was with you as you were never alone. He kept you away from gangs and bullies, that's how his love was shown. Even if you do have a lapse of judgment, you now have the tools to get back on track and recover fully. When you allow, and accept Him in your life, it becomes uncomfortable to be deceitful, diabolical, or hypocritical, living that type of lifestyle that invites strife.

With all of that in mind, you must approach life wisely and safely, while waiting more patiently and most definitely spiritually. When you obtain this, it's real. There's no adjective that will describe how you'll feel by gaining, absorbing, and consuming this knowledge. So, you can pursue that ultimate goal and attend college. Congratulations, you scored the winning run after crossing home plate; you're getting a thorough education, that's a walk-off home run. You are also receiving beneficial nutrition and quality confidential mentoring. Now that you have the truth and respect, you've achieved wellness and that's worth commemorating. Again, congratulations!

11. BLACK MANAGERS

Owners, you resemble a funeral procession, as you appear to be heading back towards the great depression. With the appearance that you're content in taking this unforeseen and unexpected nosedive, can you explain how you intend to compete and survive? The product that you're featuring is racially biased which affects minorities. In turn, it creates and produces disparity through and from the lack of equality. We almost went into the year 2016 without a Black manager being hired; this hasn't happened since 1987.

Comically speaking, the culprits responsible for these egregious actions won't be able to own a team in Heaven. As in the NFL, they have what they call the *Rooney Rule*. It states that all 30 teams must interview someone of a minority descent. Would the owners of Major League Baseball accept a proposal like that, and possibly be satisfied and content? Meanwhile, these were my feelings prior to the signing of Dave Roberts. Shame on the organization who rid us of that initial racial duplicity. The Los Angeles Dodgers, yes, I find them hesitantly guilty.

Now you've gone butt-backwards as well with your newly acquired attitude. From having the utmost of aptitude, pride, guts, and heritage being displayed in its greatest magnitude. The honor to wear and bleed Dodger blue, but not demonstrating it by not hiring long-time stars and organizational type players such as Dusty Baker nor Davey Lopes. I just can't imagine their amount of anticipation and stress, as well as their unhealthy amount of hope. That's comparable to an impatient addict waiting on his connection for dope. I'm having a hard time digesting and accepting this to be painfully true.

After the signing of Dave Roberts to the Los Angeles Dodgers, now you deserve somewhat of a reprieve. This is significantly important to proceed without further ado. This would illustrate some prosperity and out of curiosity being that Magic Johnson is part owner. How much of the decision to hire Dave Roberts came from you? Magic, are you experiencing some of the props and perks that the other owners are enjoying? Such privileges as employing by acts of nepotism? Also, don't forget about Willie Randolph, as he took the New York Mets to within one game of the 2008 World Series. This simply stinks of racism and a bunch of well-deceived theories.

If you're not strong enough, theoretically the repetitiveness of this redundancy can result in one becoming extremely drained and left weary. In the meantime, they all should sue for collusion. It's been done before, it's nothing new. These decisions aren't based on good old sound baseball knowledge with successful lineage as results. The old school White people in the front offices with intelligence are tired of enduring the doubt and insults. Now the game is evolving into analytics and sabermetrics, (started by the Oakland A's on methods of prospect selection).

Sabermetrics is the empirical analysis of baseball especially baseball statistics that measure in game activity. The old White people with the baseball knowledge are being replaced with the younger White people, who are getting hired, and are coming from an exclusive Ivy League College. Again, more evidence of the visual machination in its rapidly escalating state which trickles down determining and diminishing ethnic and minority opportunities for jobs at an alarming rate. Like most corporations, there is a form of age discrimination which effects applicants or employees over the age of forty. With that said, there goes a position of knowledge, salary and authority. While your chances are slim to none for getting hired, or maintaining employment, or more importantly, retaining it, if you're a minority.

MLB, you can no longer pretend to have a blind eye. You have, in my mind, as well as many others' minds, a major issue. After becoming aware of your dilemma, you can't cry, because we don't issue tissue. Because of this, you don't get a pass, and we can't dismiss you. If indeed you take this fall, just remember there is no crying in baseball. Sports can address controversial views and even bring change about social issues.

In this most recent case at the University of Missouri, the Black students had claims of experiencing subtle racism. One student, through his due diligence, went on a hunger strike which proved to be extremely affective and most of all prudent. Vanity was meekly dethroned by some overwhelming and powerful unity. It appeared they were backed by a large, peaceful, and an energetic community. Some surprising, but some were the most needed members of the faculty. The students deemed the president of the university unfit. Upon the students' requests, he signed his resignation without much hesitation and immediately quit. As I would be remiss, not to relish and gloat in the university's students victorious bliss. Owners, don't forget about the empty seats in Baltimore's ballpark as demonstrated just last year.

The Heavenly Father works in mysterious ways. As this most recent incident, along with the many others, specifically regarding young Black brothers. These incidents aren't accidents; they were made from God for us as people to see and hear. Owners, the minute the potential of something reminiscent of that happening to you should produce some level of fear. As the formula to execute this has been made quite and perfectly clear.

The effect from the exposure of baseball's racism could prove to be catastrophic. In the end for the owners, the possibility of losing ownership of your team certainly won't be considered minute nor microscopic. Owners, you must take culpability and assume the responsibility, before this becomes mentally excruciating, exhausting, and vehement.

Don't forget what happened to ex-LA Clippers' owner, Mr. Robert Sterling, of the NBA. His racial statements resulted in the league's punishment and his team was taken away.

Owners—here's a word of advice, think twice because it's inevitable you're potentially inducing your own judgment day. The outcome could be punishable and applicable through the Commissioner of the Court. The ultimate decision would be the absolute total termination and/or resignation from the sport. Or would you have the arrogance and the audacity to make an attempt with a prideful and egotistical retort? This duplicitous plot, in my eyes, has reached its peak. Racism is a difficult enemy to critique, its purpose is to reduce you as a human being, to become meek and weak. This may sound insensitive, as well as it being despicable. You appear to be well out of touch, and it's about time for this mission to abort. Facetiously speaking, you're doing way too much. It's the edifice that's no longer imposing that window of opportunity that you exercised and abused through degradation and manipulation is slowly closing. Your most recent racial debacle was about the failed attempt to sign and obtain Manager Bud Black. This has become habitual, which is why I'm so vitriol.

Did the Washington Nationals illustrate some moral compass? Or did ownership attempt to deceive and camouflage a mistake in its initial and primary decision? Was the signing of the new and now possibly leery Dusty Baker an embarrassing rescission? Was it about the lack of money that the Nationals offered Bud? (Black, of course) Isn't that usually one of the main reasons for divorce?

The hiring of Dusty Baker in many people's eyes should have been the Nationals' first choice. Although this is typically the outcome and somewhat predictable for minorities with little or no voice.

This is the twenty-first century. We can no longer accept this behavior nor condone this. MLB has become one of its old clichés, a big swing and a miss. You have been surprisingly negligent and very remiss. Let's get some clarity on this lack of similarity because there is a very large and unfair disparity. You can't look someone in the face and tell them you don't hire according to race.

An example being Dusty Baker is extremely impressive and quite dignified. Along with his highly acclimated player and managerial accomplishments which makes him more than qualified. Yet he was blatantly and nearly ostracized.

So, the owners must change, compensate, and improvise. To improve upon these egregious actions, while the truth and the proof can be publicized. Can this situation be resolved or at least attempt to shrink it until it actually dissolves? The time is now for all 30 of you to confer and get this situation corrected and revised. If that were to happen, I for one, volunteer in speaking for the many that would definitely be elated and pleasantly surprised and gratified. If not, these won't be very positive images and ratings for you as owners if this were to be locally, nationally, and internationally televised. Is it more than a privilege to be a Black manager? In their case, is salary going to be the new culprit of disparity? Their compensations are minimized, which is another method being utilized to neutralize. To make the best or most effective use of a situation, opportunity, or resource is to optimize. You as owners can relate to this as your strategy is to immobilize, but with this current assessment I find myself extremely confident and revitalized.

It appears to me now, how the Heavenly Father has made it in due time in which to totally succeed and capitalize. In this case, it means to take the chance to gain an advantage from a group of people. That group of people being you the owners, and after this is finalized I pray there won't be a sequel. Simply and initially, all we ever wanted was to be treated fairly and equally.

We must obtain from the owners, a productive dialogue and not an unproductive and possibly very boring monologue. The effects of the owner's duplicitous actions are extremely hideous and mysterious. While even more, so just as equally and coincidently deleterious. Owners— the approach we're attempting to achieve and acquire is to be inclusive. Now, you are comfortably and remotely purposely being exclusive. I look forward to the day when this becomes resolved in its totality. While being executed diligently, professionally, expediently, respectfully, and conclusively, owners, you taught me first hand that when you become humbled, that's a product of humility. You begin to regain your vigorous assets and the ability to take the necessary steps to take stock and inventory of your newly found rigorous honesty.

This is my testimony at best, as being most sincerely and confidently. While hopefully achieving eloquence, with no ambiguity in my soliloquy.

12. COCAINE AND ITS DELUSIONAL PAIN

Cocaine is cunning, baffling, restricting, deceiving and conflicting. Next is denial because you say this hasn't become addicting. Initially, you become induced to cocaine, and then you become seduced by cocaine. From the mental and physical abuse, eventually, you become a recluse. When you abuse and misuse cocaine, it's almost certain you'll have serious or major health issues. If your choice of usage is to snort it up your nose, there's the possibility of destroying the cells in your mucus membranes. While snorting it up your nose, it literally is going into your brain. Now, just the visual picture can be viewed and judged to be perceived as insane. It's an epidemic or disease and physically can cause a heart attack or a stroke. What's even worse with the over indulgence of coke, is that you can eventually go broke.

The street names for cocaine are coke, in the powder form it's called White girl, and in the rock form it is called the mother pearl. Formerly known as free-basing, it's been revised and fortified into the devastating rocks presently known as "crack." Unfortunately, it's most consumed by Blacks. It's smoked and self-induced while inhaled with a pipe, its popularity coincides with the ignorance and non-deserving hype. It's mostly sold, used, and found solely and purposely in the Black communities. The drug has exposed our delinquencies, insecurities, and deficiencies. Crack is sold on many and any block, it is fast and easy to make and always in stock. It has a history dating back to the early 1970's. There was a duplicitous machination from top government officials, now we're left with the devastating and somewhat morbid residuals. This is it in a nut-shell; crack was just turning up in the U.S., the Contras were seeking funds to support their civil war in Nicaragua. While a young Black man (Rick Ross) was looking for an opportunity. Presently he's had time to reflect as a Black man, how he was just a pawn in destroying the Black communities. Jail time and disgrace weren't worth the so-called lucrative opportunities.

This was totally unexpected and we were unaware of our demise through the cocaine infestation. Our communities were strategically invaded and were put under attack. While in our communities, most can't afford the necessary life insurance policies that are needed, for example, such as Aflac. You see, the drugs hit the airstrips, then to Compton to destroy the present and future of Blacks. This is where they flipped the script while making it feasible to sell drugs and weapons to the Bloods and Crips. They continue up to the bay employing the same ploy. When the mission is accomplished, did they celebrate with joy? To finish destroying more Blacks and the as equally-hated gays.

At the time, it appeared the distribution of cocaine transpired without much police presence or enforcement. Why? Because it had the C.I.A.'s endorsement. So the C.I.A. could continue to cover up with the lies and remained blind.

Through immense interest and curiosity, a local San Jose Mercury News beat writer named Gary Webb, researched and found a shocking discovery. The knowledge that he obtained eventually led to his own death, or should I say demise, resulting from an allegedly self-inflicted gunshot which was determined to be a suicide. As this occurred eight years later, his death was inevitable, as it could have just as well been deemed a homicide. He was the first writer to uncover the C.I.A.'s involvement in trafficking of drugs and arms into the U.S. He was awarded journalist of the year for an article entitled the Dark Alliance. For that he paid the price as his life turned into a living hell. There were very few people that he could trust and tell. He and his family felt the wrath of the C.I.A. as he was followed, threatened, and harassed, possibly over a period of over eight years. This had the potential not to turn out well at all. There was no loyalty shown as his editor, and even his chief editor, basically turned their backs on him, after the C.I.A. decided to play hardball. They turned the tables and made Mr. Webb a controversial figure, as if he embellished the story. Attacking his reputability obviously, purposely, and if I may say, quite paltry. Obtaining information as to him having an affair which is adultery. The woman he was involved with committed suicide as the news was permeating throughout to everyone and everything that's significant in his life. Having an effect at home and work, he and his wife can only take so much over that amount of years. He left behind a wife and two kids, mourning with pain and tears.

Gary Webb no longer lives in fear. Through his work, came the indictment of the former Deputy Director of National Security, Oliver North. He was implicated in the Iran-Contra affair, and was forced to resign. He was selling weapons to Iran to fund the war. The Iran-Contra affair was a secret arrangement in the 1980's to provide funds to the Nicaraguans by selling arms to Iran and Contra rebels from profits gained from the cocaine and arms trafficking in U.S.

The former fiery Black California Republican Maxine Waters spoke outdoors in Compton amongst a dissatisfied and angry crowd. As she was just as vitriol and vehement in her presentation while speaking on the controversial speculation of how the C.I.A. intentionally allowed illegal drugs and arms into our Black communities with the intent to destroy lives. The C.I.A. wanted to fight a war the government didn't want. When you work in secrecy and mystery it's hard to daunt. Now the street gangs are packing heavier heat, their weapons of choice being AK47's. This is partially the reason why it appears the police don't have the equivalency and are less likely to be walking a beat. The murderous and notorious gangs kill to compete for possession of the turfs in the violent streets. This Black on Black crime from our youth makes our future look very bleak.

Cocaine is ruining our communities, robbing our youth of life's wonderfully legal and unique opportunities. As a result, the politician's actions were horrific as they were confident this plot had the potential to be very prolific. The crack is produced and man-made while they're becoming non-professionally scientific. That means they're making illegal money without education and training. Eventually, the enthusiasm for the cause will lessen, and they will be left waning. Do I need to be more specific, because it's difficult to understand that this is absolutely cryptic?

While this all took place, the United States turned a blind eye to the notorious strongman Manuel Antonio Noriega, the ruthless Panamanian military leader. He was also known as the world's biggest drug and arms cartel dealer. The powers that be, two of the biggest and richest cocaine suppliers in the U.S. One was Oscar Danilio Blandon who became a snitch against the C.I.A. as he supplied the Midwest and the East coast, specifically New York. He made an estimated six hundred billion dollars. While he supplied a Black man, glamorous Freeway Rick Ross, made an estimated six million in Los Angeles and the surrounding areas. All the while the C.I.A. let it all in the country. Those are the real criminals.

The young Blacks are underachieving due to over-

whelming circumstances. Seemingly, this is misleading
Blacks in structure and are the lowest in the operation.
They are basically the street dealers. Then you have the
suppliers, they are more so the leaders. The street dealers
that are trying to survive on the streets are blatantly treated
worse than animals. They are herding young Black males
in mass numerations into a life of politically induced incarceration. It's happening all across our politically incorrect
nation. Example being, when the criminals get caught and
arrested, they make their one phone call to their lawyer
and four hours later they're out of jail on bail. Plausibly,
never to be seen again nor sentenced, or the worst possible outcome minimally is a short sentence. They're put
under witness protection and are no longer in existence.
Now here's the great disparity—the hustler on the streets
gets busted and he or she stays in jail because they can't
afford a lawyer until they get a court date. Then, one is
given a court-appointed lawyer.

Here are some compelling statistics according to the
National Survey on Drug Use: 6.6% of White adolescents
and young adults ages 12 to 25 sold drugs, compared to
just 5% of Blacks. This is a 32% difference. In poor Black
neighborhoods drugs tend to be sold outdoors, in the
open. In White neighborhoods, by contrast, drug transac-
tions typically happen indoors, often between friends and
acquaintances. Their operations require less mental and
physical maintenance. If you sell drugs outside you're
much more likely to get caught. Unfortunately, that's a hell
of a lesson to be taught. So, we now have a better understanding of the history, the beginning, and the arrest of the
government's most wanted. The fall guy, Manuel Noriega,
is said to have been the world's biggest drug and arms cartel leader. Now at 81 years of age, he's in a wheelchair
literally sitting in jail. After all the tragedy and death he

caused, it's only proper and fitting that he endures the rest of his life in a cell—a living hell.

Through him and the government, they are partially the blame for the destruction of many Black families and other lives. The most undeserving people are the mothers and wives. The Black male historically and unfortunately has fallen prey to the evils and perils of drugs and alcohol. As your mother, wife, and kids have to witness and experience him hitting the bottom, what a fall. On the other hand, it's a rarity to separate a Black woman from her child. Without the presence of either functioning parents, most likely the child will become incarcerated and basically dangerously wild.

Crack was the evil temptation the Black woman just couldn't prevail. She lost her pride and that special will to excel. Now crack is the repetitious gateway to hell. The devastation and embarrassment to you and your family is traumatic and in some cases, catastrophic. Maybe it's possible that in your life drugs and alcohol are your main and preferred topic. This can leave you with permanent mental and physical scars. Especially if you're unavoidably detained behind bars. Now it gets compounded; incarceration is even worse when you're a celebrity or a star. What you've been hiding is exposed to the media, and now everyone knows what you do and who you are. It will be your worst experience in your life by far.

This is the scenario of a very good friend. Finally, he picked a good fight with the Lord Jesus Christ. It was time for it to end and time for a new beginning to begin. As one day, he woke up and realized he was tired of being consumed with sin, looking back at what he lost and what it cost. He reflected on when he was getting high and spent the money for rent. His wife wants to know what he's doing and where he went. When he tries to express his hurt and pain, his wife looks at him with raging anger and total disdain. Now he shamefully attempted to explain, looking for someone or something to blame. What a perfect time to man-up and admit he's powerless to cocaine, but no, a lie comes out of his mouth instead. What's really going on inside his head, now your wife has figured out the other day why your nose bled. All she can do to stop from killing you is to go lock the door to your room and cry. This is called denial and until you accept your addiction, you'll remain insane inside your brain. It appears to you all the wife does is complain. Every day you become more delusional and less compatible. As time goes on you're trying to figure out how to beat this drug, and is it even combatable? In time without clinical or medical help you won't be able to refrain, and you'll no longer be able to substantially maintain.

The most misleading aspect of cocaine is that it's a prestigious drug. One that supposedly isn't addicting, that statement alone is quite conflicting. It was considered a social drug, and that was another disputable plug.

One day I happened to be driving through the hood, I witnessed something disgusting, embarrassing, and as the millennial would say "that's totally whack." After that I wasn't particularly feeling remotely good. I witnessed and saw with my two eyes a grandmother trying to buy some crack. What hurt the most was she's more than likely someone's mother. This just must stop, between these damn drugs and our youth killing each other. Instead, we must commit to find ways to better love one another. Start having unity back in our communities, and begin to educate and celebrate our young sisters and brothers. Teach them to lead and not follow. Have some substance and become fortified, not hollow. Failure is not an option, it's derived from inadequacies, the lack of deficiencies of quali-

ty and quantity. Producing unstable insecurities and actions with the probability of immense strife in one's life.

Our characteristics are derived and solidified by star-
tling and disparaging statistics. Wow, who would have
thought, the usage of cocaine and analytics in the same
sentence! Essentially, cocaine is a cash cow economically
and it appears it will remain substantially lucrative, wow!
This powerful drug is increasingly destroying our communities and country exponentially.

I would like to express some of the effects cocaine has
had in my life personally. First, there are three things you
can look forward to when you do drugs and alcohol: hospitalization, incarceration, and death, and quite frankly that
was enough for me. I had already done two out the three.
I felt like a boxer getting knocked down, and taking a
standing eight count on one knee. But a knockout isn't
what I foresee. This won't be left up to the referee. It's
time to stop asking yourself why me. Your actions are becoming critical and they're no longer beneficial. They have
gone from being respectful and almost impeccable to being irresponsible, embarrassing, and unprofessional. You
socialize with leeches and they suck you dry and hang
around you like debris.

Did I enjoy it? If I said yes would that be an indication
that I'm sick—maybe. Hospitalization is what I perceive as
clinical. After two D.U.I.'s a year apart, and with the possession of cocaine that led to incarceration, which in turn
led to hospitalization. I was sent to drug and alcohol rehab
four different times, partially for committing D.U.I. crimes.
This is immaturity compounded with addiction, these actions are detrimental and at this rate you won't make into
your prime. It was basically mandatory applicable by the
team and the courts. You're troubled and now labeled and
disabled. This time it was not for the team or courts to send

me; it was time to become free and return to the man I was meant to be. With the levels and degrees of shame, there was doubt if I'd ever pitch in another big league game. Will I be able to take care of my family financially and how much remains? Will I still be respected and admired the same? Will it leave a blemish on my career and fame? The mental anguish of if I would have, if I could have, and if I should have? The reality that things may never be the same, I have no one, but myself to blame. You can't even look in the mirror without feeling remorse and shame! Although through all my detriment, sobriety is what I 'm able to honestly proclaim.

After my Heavenly Father and family, nothing is more important to me than my sobriety. In order to accomplish and succeed, you must work diligently to make it a priority. Through my Heavenly Father, I became a father eighteen years ago. I prayed for wisdom and I received it along with knowledge and sobriety. My daughter is my inspiration and motivation to contribute gallantly to impact society. I continue to strengthen my identity and fortify my domain. He's blessed me with so much knowledge, that it's hard to contain. I will continue to exist, endure, persist, prevail, curtail, survive, and stay alive. Getting rid of this lifestyle had to be done. I just couldn't stay up another night again, until I've seen the sun. That did it, that was the last straw, being in the company of a fool with a gun. I knew this had to be over. I needed drastically, desperately and clarity to get sober.

I'm going to close with this, as I must explain. I've found that you need spirituality. Who is my Heavenly Father to fight all my battles against the evils in life effectively? If need be, with it proven to bring stress and strife, in your life in which are the synonyms and symptoms, such as friction, controversy, dispute, conflict, and discord. All that dysfunction in one's life; this you just can't afford. The lack of harmony and you're no longer in tune with your spirituality. Was I paranoid? Were my actions and activities becoming detectable? I was so obsessed with the lifestyle that I couldn't even get down on my knees and pray, and that's not acceptable. Was it okay? No how and no way.

In my opinion, it's a form of Satan, and my approach is that I tell him to get behind me in Jesus' precious name. "One must stay devoid of Satan's continuity and all his futility." *Matthew Chapter 4*. In the Bible, the Heavenly Father teaches that "Satan won't be amongst those that make it into eternity." *Revelation Chapter 20.*

The Heavenly Father also teaches in biblical times about sorcery and wizardry, which pertains to drugs in today's time in *Revelations Chapter 21 verse 8*, which states, "But the fearful and unbelieving, and the abominable, and murderers, and whoremongers and sorcerers and idolaters and all liars, shall have their part in the lake which burns fire and brimstone; which is the second death." This last scripture, *Titus Chapter 2-7* teaches how the whole family should be sober. I pray for everyone, those who are sober to stay sober and those who aren't please try a little harder to get sober, before it's over!

13. GLENN BURKE, THE FIRST OPENLY GAY BALL PLAYER

Is he gay
Can he play
Do management and the front office care
Will they judge him based on his sexuality
In a politically correct society is that fair

Playing with the first openly gay
Baseball player to come out
As I look back, there's no doubt
He lost that bout

Where there are rumors
there are lies and some truth

But unless you see it
there is no proof

Coming off the road after 14 days
Everybody gets picked up by a wife or girlfriend

Not him – his man picked him up
They were two men
Who were openly gay

Even though you still didn't know
He was a bully growing up
So he was very macho

A very loyal teammate, he was
He'd be the first
To be there if it were time to fight

But after the game
a quick shower and gone into the night
He knows everyone was uncomfortable in the showers
So he showered first and was gone in less than half an
hour

Now what happens when you're all alone in the shower
And you find out not only are you homophobic
But now you've become claustrophobic

Your parents raised you up with teachings from the Bible
And you are taught homosexuality is an abomination

Wake up son; it's 2017
Gays have the same rights
As you all across the wonderful nation

Pro sports is the last profession
To openly accept gays in the workplace

Well it looks like this issue is going
To continually stare them right in the face

He was a great guy and smart
With a super sense of humor

But when he came out
It was no longer a rumor

He was my friend
All the way
To the end

As he got HIV and became sick
Now he's RIP
Rest in peace my brother
Will there ever be another

14. THE TIME IS NOW

Pride - that's what we had regarding our Black athletes
who paved the way.
Joe Louis, Jackie Robinson and back then, Cassius Clay.
God has sent a reawakening that presently came our way.

How ironic that Jackie Robinson became iconic
He has intimate memories with Blacks and other platonic
His legacy has persevered, as he has become totally
revered
Presently there is a Black team from Chicago that wears
his brand and logo.

Who became the best little league team in the nation?
It was beautiful as they were great in their presentation,
And were an absolute total inspiration.

Most were well-spoken and extremely composed
So it shows they're paying attention to get their education
It's obvious from their play they have immense dedication.

Then there was Mo'ne
You missed something if you didn't see her play.

That's right I said her!
Who throws the ball so fast it looks like a blur?

She is one of the best pitchers in the nation
She is truly one of God's wonderful creations

Yes she can hurl with the best in the world
She made history as the first little leaguer
To make the cover of Sports Illustrated

Thanks, Mo'ne Davis
You're highly appreciated.

She sure is as Major League Baseball
has put her jersey in the Hall of Fame
That's how much impact she had on the game.

This has validated my commitment to our youth through baseball as the vehicle to promote education, mentoring and nutrition in order to achieve wellness.

I have a traveling baseball league for ages eight through eleven. Presently, I'm targeting Antioch, Pittsburg, Richmond, Oakland, Bay Point, Mt. Diablo, San Pablo, Vallejo, Berkeley, and Concord, as those cities can gain access to this wonderful after-school program known as the Mike Norris School of Baseball and Wellness. If you are a city interested in our program, check out our website link below.

Unfortunately, the reality we deal with in underprivileged communities is crime and lack of education. Tackling these two issues is essential to the success of one's life. Our program is designed to address dysfunctional behaviors that can lead to incarceration or death. One out of three Black youth statistically will be incarcerated in their lifetime. Could this be another reason why this may be contributing to the lack of African-Americans in Major League Baseball? Education is the key to prosperity.

By eight years old, a child must start to create an environment that's conducive to education or they begin to fall behind in a society being built on economics which determines your value! Failing in the school system is almost certain incarceration. The value of education is as simple as this, when you get to high school, you must obtain a certain grade point average to play your sport of choice.

One third are lost to poor grades. If you're good enough to play in college, you also must pass your classes to be eligible. If you're good enough professionally, but you have no aspirations to go to college, you might have cost yourself millions of dollars. On the other hand, if you have a 3.0 grade point average with intentions of going to college, your stock goes up millions of dollars. College is your leverage and bargaining piece. Economics and politics, the youth know nothing about.

America's corporations, if you saw the Little League World Series, you witnessed sixteen young Black males who have survived living in the murder capital of the nation, Chicago, Illinois. There were 561 murders last year. These sixteen young Black males overcame abnormal circumstances and extreme temptations brought an entire city, as well as the nation, together and that was beyond great!

In Oakland, there are 400 or more little leaguers playing baseball, between three leagues: Cal Ripken, RBI, and Babe Ruth. This makes Oakland a great tradition of baseball, the mecca, so to speak, in the Bay Area. Such greats as Frank Robinson, Vada Pinson, Curt Flood, Joe Morgan, Rickey Henderson, Bip Roberts, Dave Stewart, and Lloyd Moseby. I also have ex-major leaguers to assist in coaching – such names as Vida Blue, Bip Roberts, Shooty Babitt, Claudell Washington, Al Woods, Brian Guinn, Tiny Fielder, Rich Murray, Ed Miller, and minor leaguers, as well as college and high school coaching. Youths will be provided with gloves and uniforms and best of all, it is free!

They will be given paper, pen and pencils for afterschool tutoring, and nutritional snacks on Mondays and Wednesdays, and a home cooked meal on Friday Family Night. Bring an adult, preferably a parent. There will be a barbeque after every game. Each youth will have educational learning tools made available to them. There will be prizes to be won by answering the trivia questions from the learning tools correctly. In conclusion, they must comprehend this – born a male but being a man is by choice!

Please visit my website at www.apitchtosuccess.com for more comprehensive information and just pure enjoyment.

Corporate America, there is no money available in our communities to help one another. Help is desperately needed. Lives are at stake, our future as a nation is at stake. This isn't getting any better. These are innocent, pure children who shouldn't have to fear drive-by shootings, drug selling on every corner, prostitution, almost hopeless family structures, and babies raising babies. This is where our mentoring program will be; the other essential key as well as the nutrition and tutoring. All of this is the goal to fruition for wellness.

God Bless!

15. PRESIDENT BARACK OBAMA

He became the 44th and first Black President in the history of this nation. His astonishing victory was amazing despite many of the potential voters that were dismissive or hesitant. His message was expressing and proclaiming change. This is what he promised people which covered a wide range—gays, Mexican immigrants, young White Americans, and Black Americans. Had you been born over 40 years ago; all this change would appear to be odd or strange.

This fearless leader passed progressive laws and bills on Capitol Hill. As promised, he addressed and accomplished basically all his goals and more through God's merciful will. We're now well aware that there is same-sex marriage, the legalization of marijuana in 14 states, and his birthing of Obama-Care. Obama put in an executive action for deportation protection, where Mexican immigrants could receive a three-year work permit. This can affect 4 million unauthorized immigrants. Now they can no longer be victimized, nor treated like someone with no significance.

I truly never thought I'd live to see, a Black man voted into the highest-ranking office in the nation, the presidency. Mr. President, you exhibited the ability all over the world that if you can perceive, conceive, and ultimately achieve. Through spite to victorious despite, you won that fight. As a

Democratic president, you beat up that conflicting Republican elephant.

Just recently, through one of the most horrific events to my knowledge, the church murders in South Carolina. A young White male murdered defenseless innocent Black people apparently ignorant to racism. Mr. President, you transformed into the late great Dr. Martin Luther King Jr., as you achieved one of your finest moments in your presidency giving the eulogy. You managed to turn something into beautiful that was so tragic and ugly.

You are why Blacks can say I'm Black and I'm proud! As the late, great James Brown said, "Say it loud!" I wish people like Dr. King, Malcolm X, Huey Newton, and James Brown could have lived long enough to see you become president. Mr. Brown died one year before you were elected. Perhaps the names I mentioned would have appreciated your history making most, that's why they were selected.

When you took office, this country was financially, morally, and politically bankrupt. Now it doesn't appear to be so blatantly corrupt. Osama bin Laden, you captured and disposed of America's most wanted. You extremely exhausted him as you hunted, haunted and daunted him before he was expounded. You're doing a well-respected and an exceptional job worldwide, working towards obtaining peace in the Middle East. Also, making a tactical move involving our European allies that are essentially on America's side and making an effort for ISIS to subside.

You're an exceptional leader and role model for young and old. A great husband and father, let that story be told. Behind every strong man is a strong woman, but Mr. President, you exceeded yourself. The First Lady has class, grace, beauty, dignity, charm, elegance, and most but not least, intelligence. You are an enviable and admirable individual. A man with an impeccable master plan. Mr. President, you obtained, you maintained, and you sustained, but what's most impressive has been your ability to ascertain. What brilliance, composure, charm, class, etiquette, and swag. When you have all of this going for you, it must be hard not to brag. We haven't had a president like you in quite a while with your integrity. Thanks for eight exceptional years, but after you're gone this is my fear. That Americans will experience gravity. Will the Office of the Presidency turn into a calamity? What goes up must come down. I don't want this wonderful story to end with a frown. I hope and rigorously pray that our next president won't be about promises that turn into lies. You've restored the economy, but after you leave do Americans again watch and become powerless as the economy dies? Will the next president be transparent and hollow? Mr. President, you are and will be a tough act to follow!

16. TO THE DISABLED— DON'T ACCEPT BEING LABELED

Thanks to the considerate and caring people who had enough compassion, when they saw me approaching, they stopped and assisted me by opening the door. To the immense amount of times I've fallen and couldn't get up, and someone was there to pick me up off the floor. After dusting yourself off, you thank God you didn't get hurt any worse, not in need for a doctor or nurse. At times, you wish you didn't have to go through this agony anymore, but I look at it as temporary and that I'm doing God's chore! I live every day with faith and an abundance of enthusiasm, therefore, life is never a bore. Life becomes just a routine task, and when you need to get out of difficulty when you pray to God, just ask.

This is what I suggest, and I must confess, faith is the key to your life's success. Staying positive will abridge being negative. With that attitude, people don't want to be around you if it's repetitive. Even when you're disabled, you can still be an example in a positive way. When people see a smile on your face, just by you saying hi and have a nice day. That person becomes touched, and now it's a different perception they have of you. Instead of the feeling of empathy and sympathy, now it's an automatic respect they pay. This can motivate them to have something nice to say.

Now, perhaps you've made their day after the class and courage you display and portray. Now, do you see how much power you have without using it physically, it mostly comes from being strong mentally and spiritually. Disabilities come in many different forms, to be blind, deaf, or even paralyzed. To be presumed permanent and finished; a definitive version of finalized.

You may have a physical disability, but your mind isn't immobilized. Disabled to you should mean don't let yourself be defined or labeled. Continue to pray for your condition to get better or go away. It won't hurt to make a concerted effort to pray every day. That's why God made doctors, so that they can come up with a cure. With faith and modern medicine, to procure is what you need for sure. God gives you the strength, courage, and tools with the ability to fight and endure. Just always remember that winners never quit and quitters never win! You must begin, in order to get to the end. Spiritually speaking, when you repent of your sins, this is another effective and the most powerful way to win. Amen! Get rid of the jealousy and envy as God can let the good blessings in.

(Amen: this Hebrew word in the old testament means "so be it".) *Revelation 3:14*

MIKE NORRIS

49661104R00104

Made in the USA
San Bernardino, CA
01 June 2017